NEA
SCHOOL RESTRUCTURING SERIES

Portfolio Practices

Thinking Through The Assessment of Children's Work

Steve Seidel
Joseph Walters

Edward Kirby
Nina Olff
Kimberly Powell
Larry Scripp
Shirley Veenema

The APPLE Project
Project Zero
Harvard Graduate School of Education

Robert M. McClure
Series Editor

An NEA Professional Library Publication
National Education Association
Washington, D.C.

CONTENTS

Dedicated to Elliot Tocci, educator and friend
1943-1996

FOREWORD

The search for effective ways to capture evidence of students' academic growth began when teacher first met child. Sometimes the search focuses on the need to help people outside of the classroom know about a child's progress. Other times it grows from a need to describe how all students in a classroom are doing—or all students in a school or district or state. In these efforts, we've grown increasingly sophisticated with our psychometric tools, capturing with numbers plotted against predetermined standards where students are in relation to where they should be.

Other efforts focus on assessment techniques that describe student accomplishment with an eye toward the assessment itself making a direct contribution to the acts of learning and teaching. These efforts range from the very informal (teacher questioning during discussions, for example) to the more formal (assessing accomplishments through rubrics).

This book is about both kinds of efforts—outside and inside, if you will. It is a remarkable endeavor in the way it provides very practical ideas for teachers to use as they help students plan, collect, analyze, and present their work. It also gives teachers and others in schools language they can use to help others understand and value portfolios. Students and their families will benefit greatly from this work. Teachers' effectiveness will improve as they implement the ideas presented here.

The book also helps those of us who wish that people outside of everyday contact with teaching and learning could experience the richness and excitement of schooling. It is important that policy-makers, the press, and others know how students are progressing as measured against standards set by them. But it is also important to know how students are making their own sense of the academic disciplines they are learning. What logic informs their learning? What order do they make of history or science or music? What reasoning do they employ in their writing or debating? What is their sense of beauty?

Using the products of their learning to understand their learning is a powerful way to improve educational opportunities for students. It is also a powerful way to help students become more skillful and independent in their own learning.

Well-conceived student assessment practices are at the heart of quality schooling. *Portfolio Practices: Thinking Through the Assessment of Children's Work* will make a significant contribution to those involved in restructuring their curriculum, pedagogical practices, and the organizational and cultural dimensions of their schools.

—Robert M. McClure, Series Editor

PREFACE

This work was supported by generous grants from the Rockefeller Foundation, the Lilly Endowment, the Four Seasons Project, and The Pew Charitable Trusts. Judy Pace and Mindy Kornhaber were original members of the APPLE research group at Project Zero. Howard Gardner was the senior advisor. We thank them and all of our colleagues at Project Zero for their many contributions to the project and to this book.

We also thank Barbara Berns and Adria Steinberg for their wise editorial counsel.

We are most grateful to Joan Lipsitz for her perspective and support throughout the years of the project. Finally, we are especially grateful to the teachers and administrators who have collaborated with us on this work over the past five years. While many of the individuals are quoted in the text, the following list also acknowledges their schools and communities:
- Fuller School, Gloucester, Massachusetts
- Gorham Maine Public Schools, Gorham, Maine
- Graham & Parks Alternative School, Cambridge, Massachusetts
- Marion Selzer School, Cleveland, Ohio
- Rindge School of Technical Arts, Cambridge, Massachusetts
- Shutesbury Elementary School, Shutesbury, Massachusetts
- The Agnon School, Beachwood, Ohio
- The Atrium School, Watertown, Massachusetts
- The Eakin School, Nashville, Tennessee
- The Key School, Indianapolis, Indiana
- University School, Shaker Heights, Ohio
- Veterans Memorial Elementary School, Provincetown, Massachusetts

INTRODUCTION

Before you even open Tasha's portfolio, you see the four paintings that are too big for the folder. The edges are getting dog-eared but lay them out on the table and you have a stunning picture of what her neighborhood looks like to this nine year old—the buildings that shine, those that need fixing, the people who smile and those who just stare. Start flipping through her work and you'll find pages from her math notebook that reveal not only the answers to the problems but her explanations of how she thought through her search for solutions. Keep going and find her reader's journal with three entries she's marked as ones she wants you to read because they will tell you important things about her as a reader. There are photos of her science project because it was too big to put in a folder and the plants all died anyway, a video-tape of the play she helped to write and acted in, two stories and three poems.

This work wasn't everything she made in school this year. Tasha selected what she felt would give a good picture of her most important work and her teacher, Ms. Davis, reviewed her choices, encouraging her to add the paintings. Ms. Davis also added some brief written comments to the collection and a description of each of the major projects the class had done so you could get a sense of how these pieces of work reflect the curriculum.

Over the past ten years, interest has been growing in the use of portfolios for the assessment of student learning and, ultimately, of the effectiveness of educational programs. The idea is quite simple. Instead of having children take tests to determine what they are learning, teachers examine and assess their essays, stories, math proofs, science experiments, plays, and on and on.

WHY PORTFOLIOS? (IF PORTFOLIOS ARE THE ANSWER, WHAT'S THE PROBLEM?)

As more and more teachers have adapted some of the major curriculum innovations of the last decades—for example, whole language, process writing, the use of manipulatives in mathematics, and cooperative learning—they have experienced a serious problem. Tests, especially the standardized and multiple choice varieties, are limited and inflexible in what and how they measure. These new approaches to curriculum and instruction encourage students to be active learners, working in groups, learning through trial and error, interaction, and the solution of complex problems and tasks. Most tests fall far short of measuring complex, multi-dimensional work, and grades don't report on progress and growth.

Teachers are frustrated. They engage children in new approaches to curriculum but have no way to measure the qualities that are most important. They want assessments that value the work children do on their many assignments. When tests are what counts, children stop believing in the importance of the other school work they do. Grades also are inadequate. They further deflate the value children place in their work. Teachers want children and parents, administrators and school boards to respect the unpredictable patterns, struggles and accomplishments of the learning process. But how to document learning? How to show evidence of the complex weave of thinking, practicing, investigating, making and doing that mark a child's growth and development in school?

Frustration and dissatisfaction are often the starting points for changes in any classroom practice. When a teacher becomes frustrated with the lack of freedom her students have to move around the classroom and work easily with each other, she begins to redesign the space and, often, the tasks she assigns. Another teacher's feeling that his students are not getting enough time to really investigate questions they've raised may lead him to radically rethink how many topics he will cover in his curriculum. This is certainly true of assessment as well. Among the many frustrations teachers have with standardized tests, the fact that they provide no information about how a child approaches her work or names and solves problems is high on the list. This frustration, as well as others, has led many teachers to try using portfolios.

Dissatisfaction, in itself, may provide new clues about changes to try; and frustrations provide the motivation for change. But it is only through careful analysis of current practice that teachers can make a practical and systematic plan for change. Using portfolios is demanding work that requires both dissatisfaction with current approaches to assessment and, also, clarity about what assessment should and could do—what information it should produce for students, teachers and parents and how it can stimulate growth and learning.

Work with portfolios appears promising and many teachers have started to use them. For the last decade Project Zero researchers, in initiatives like Arts Propel and the APPLE project, have been working with dozens of those teachers, just like Ms. Davis, in elementary and secondary schools, public and private. Together we have explored the use of portfolios as a learning experience and an assessment tool. Much of what we have seen is full of promise—and challenges. In this volume, we present some conclusions from almost a decade of research on portfolios and outline some of the challenges of using them on a school-wide basis.

SOME PROMISES

Students Develop Habits of Self-assessment

In too many schools, student work is disposable. Teachers give assignments. Students hand in their work. It is graded, returned, glanced at, and all too often forgotten, lost, or thrown in a box never to be looked at again. In portfolio classrooms the things children make are saved and revisited throughout the year. Students are asked to think and write or talk about their own assessments of their work. Of course, teachers express their opinions, too. But the children's perspectives are critical if, ultimately, they are to become their own most rigorous and sophisticated critics.

Conversations about what makes for quality work are common in portfolio classrooms. What does quality look like? What could you aim for? How does your work compare to the work of others? What are a work's unique features? Models are examined and analyzed. The makers of accomplished pieces are interviewed about their creative processes. The work of assessment is opened up and made explicit to everyone.

A Picture of Learning Emerges

As portfolios begin to fill up, a picture of learning emerges. Over time, it becomes clear how a child is—or isn't—achieving mastery of the skills and processes being practiced as well as the evolution of ideas. In kindergarten, self portraits drawn in October, January and May reveal a child's emerging control of the pencil, developing capacity to represent the human body and evolving expressions of the child's image of herself. In middle school, reading journals chronicle the development of a student's taste in literature and capacity to make sense of complex writing. In high school, an analytic report on surveys of teenagers' opinions on controversial topics document a student's increasingly sophisticated grasp of methods for data analysis.

In each of these portfolios, there are highly individual portraits of children. They are not easy to read. They take time and thought and benefit from conversation and re-reading, much more like a complex novel than an article in *Reader's Digest*.

Parents See Their Children as Learners

Traditionally, parent conferences are occasions for parents to sit with their child's teacher and hear a litany of test scores. The grade book is consulted frequently and cited as evidence of the child's performance. When children have created portfolios of their work, there is a radically different basis for conversations in these conferences. The teacher can refer directly to the pieces in the collection to provide evidence of the child's efforts, growth and accomplishments. If comparisons are important for clarifying how the child's work relates to that of her peers, then work of children of comparable age and background can be brought out.

Teachers report that parents—after reading over their child's portfolio—often have valuable stories and distinct perspectives to add to the teacher's understanding of the child as a learner. They also report that after several conferences with portfolios on the table, many parents stop asking for test scores and even pay far less attention to grades, preferring to talk about the work itself.

Teacher Conversations Focus on Student Work

It is almost unheard of in schools for teachers to talk together about the assessment of children's work. The specific analysis of the stories children write or the ways they solve complex mathematical problems is almost never a part of a teacher's day, month or year. Many teachers spend their entire careers without participating in any form of collaborative assessment. More and more, however, portfolios are providing a basis for conversations among teachers about the quality of student work. Project Zero researchers have been especially concerned with engaging teachers in close readings of children's work to see how much we can come to understand about the child and the work. Having looked carefully at the work, we try to describe what we have seen. We consider all of the questions the work raises for us about the specific child, children in general, work in particular domains, the effectiveness of certain curriculum, and more. We speculate on what the child was working on (in addition to or beside the assignment). And we talk at length about ways to help the child extend learning and continue making new works.

MEETING THE CHALLENGES OF PORTFOLIO ASSESSMENT

Portfolio assessment is not a simple activity. It is far more complicated than assigning a grade to a piece of student writing, a math test or a report card at the end of the term. But it also has the potential to be far more satisfying and useful for students, teachers and parents. The move to portfolio assessment is a move to build a school community around the thoughtful examination and celebration of student work. When students are given complex and thought-provoking assignments, they are likely to produce complex and thought-provoking work. These products can become the center of many conversations between teachers and students, students and parents, teachers and parents, teachers and their colleagues and administrators. These works can illustrate what individual children have done as well as what the school looks for in the work of all students.

Neither the practice of portfolio assessment nor the transition from other forms of assessment to portfolios is straightforward or smooth. Every teacher and every school starting to work with portfolios encounters challenges. Teacher isolation, class size and the inflexibility of schedules are common obstacles. Confusion about the language of assessment and the theoretical basis for assessments must be discussed, sorted through and clarified. The challenges are inherent in working with portfolios and the obstacles are almost inevitable when changing such a fundamental aspect of classroom life. These challenges and obstacles can be exciting and invigorating or frustrating and overwhelming (or all of the above) depending on a school staff's readiness to take on the complex work of making these changes.

PORTFOLIO PRACTICES

Our research has convinced us that nearly all of the problems and challenges inherent in work with portfolios can be anticipated and prepared for in a series of reflective "portfolio practices." The successful implementation of portfolios requires considerable attention, collaboration and creativity on the part of a school staff, including administrators, teachers, aides, department coordinators and all other adults who work with the children or care for the school. These portfolio practices require staff to engage in a variety of structured and regular activities. Some are designed to set direction for teaching and learning in the school. Others are for the professional development demanded by alternative assessments. And others are designed to ensure that there is an atmosphere in the school conducive to change. These practices require that:

- staff have time to meet and talk about the directions they want to go with curriculum and assessment;
- teachers experiment with new curricular and assessment practices in their classrooms in an ongoing way;
- teachers, parents, administrators, and students assess the assessments themselves for their educational value (the usefulness of the information they give to students and teachers);
- regular staff time is devoted to careful, collaborative assessment of student work; and
- teachers examine classroom practice and educational theories and explore the relationship between the two.

Changes in practice and school structure must be discussed, demonstrated or otherwise shared with parents, district administrators and community members. Small faculty study groups, full faculty meetings, open houses for parents, and newsletters will help to explain the portfolio process. Teachers also need to share developments in their practice with colleagues in other schools, both within and across districts.

No school is likely to do all of these practices at once and there is no precise order in which they should be done. They are meant to be used by each school's staff in a way that makes sense for that staff. They should all be considered, however, since each of the practices was designed to address specific problems and challenges that emerge through work with portfolios.

WHAT ARE REFLECTIVE PRACTICES?

The practices we are suggesting create time and space for a conscious stepping back from daily routines to look carefully with colleagues at classroom and school-wide assessment practices, to examine the effectiveness of those assessments and to consider improvements. It is a time to take a hard look, to gather ideas and information that will inform discussion and to make tentative conclusions. Careful listening, frequent summarizing, clarifying differences of perspective and opinion, and classifying problems, issues and ideas are some key features of these practices.

These practices are just that—things to practice. They are not one-shot activities. They must be engaged in over and over, time after time. They must become a part of the life of the school.

This kind of work is both very familiar and quite uncommon in most schools. Individual teachers analyze what is happening in their classrooms all the time. They make countless decisions based on those analyses and their accumulated experience. Usually this process takes place almost entirely in a teacher's head—alone and silently. (In team-teaching situations, happily, this is often not the case.) Both the sporadic and the private nature of most teachers' self-assessments severely limits the impact of those assessments on school-wide evaluation or improvements. In short, teachers often make significant changes in their classrooms, but those changes may have little or no influence on the rest of the school. Other teachers benefit from neither the successes nor failures of their colleagues' classroom innovations.

With these practices, we are advocating a series of shifts in this process—from a teacher's internal monologue to a public conversation, from lingering frustrations to plans for experiments, from something new in one classroom that others may never know about to a collective endeavor in which analysis leads to planning, experimenting and evaluation of those experiments.

FROM INDIVIDUAL CLASSROOMS TO WHOLE SCHOOLS

Unfortunately, much of the best work being done with portfolios is in isolated classrooms or pockets of classrooms in schools where otherwise there has been little change in the ways assessment is conducted. In our collaborations with teachers, we have encountered serious problems in the attempt to implement portfolios on a school-wide basis. Preeminent among these difficulties is the fact that most teachers are terribly isolated with little or no opportunity for sustained and serious conversation with their colleagues about student work or the educational effectiveness of their classroom practices. Even less common is the opportunity to visit other schools to see innovative, or just different, approaches to curriculum, instruction and assessment. (Professional development cannot occur if the professionals never have opportunities to talk to each other.)

Closed Doors/Open Doors

Closed doors characterize the isolation of most teachers in American schools. In school, after school we have seen how teachers tend to keep their work—and the work of their students—hidden from public view. Teachers don't visit each others' classrooms. Visitors may be welcome but are not usually encouraged. There is a preference for privacy about what is happening in the classrooms of most schools.

Perhaps the most insidious consequence of a 'closed door' culture is that it becomes almost impossible to have serious conversations about what is really happening behind those doors—what kind of teaching and learning is really taking place. If we don't come together to look hard at what students are doing and making, thinking and saying, we have a very difficult time making rational and thoughtful improvements. In order to make change possible, we believe the doors to classrooms have to open.

Talking About Teaching and Learning

If schools are to become places where conversations about teaching and learning occur, opportunities for those conversations must be created—among teachers themselves, as well as among teachers, children, and parents. Of course, we must go further and add administrators from within the building and from within the district as well as other members of the community who care about the children and the school. In other words, there must be regular and frequent conversation among all the participants in any child's schooling.

But what is all this talk about? It's a way to think deeply and with others about teaching and learning, and to draw ideas for strengthening each participant as a learner and the school as a learning environment. There are three kinds of conversations that need to go on among teachers in order to provoke, sustain, and ground deep thinking. These are:

- conversations about student work;
- conversations about new practices teachers try in their classrooms;
- conversations about the language and ideas of teaching and learning that underlie what is done in the classroom.

Conversations between students, teachers, and parents are similar, in many ways, to those among teachers. Often they are:

- grounded in looking at the student work and student reflections in portfolios;
- focused on identifying student interests, questions, concerns, and growth;
- aimed at learning more about the student as a learner and ways in which school can become a more effective learning environment;
- focused on how everyone can contribute to increasing the value of the child's learning experience.

This book is about creating structures and opportunities for these conversations.

THREE PRINCIPLES FOR THESE PRACTICES

Three principles have guided the development of our portfolio practices.

1. Put Student Learning as the Highest Priority for Assessments

We believe that assessment, like curriculum, should be designed with the primary purpose of providing a learning experience for students and teachers. With portfolios, students become actively engaged in understanding the quality, progress and effort of their work. Portfolios also enable teachers to have a better sense of what their students are learning, how they are learning, and how to help them in that process. Parents also can become more actively involved in the assessment process with portfolios, allowing them to contribute perspective, information, observations, and questions. Portfolio assessment provides wonderful opportunities to focus on the actual work that children do.

2. Work with the Whole School—All Students, All Staff, and as Many Parents as Possible

Project Zero's previous research indicated that there were many problems with the integration of portfolio assessment when only a few teachers in a school served as portfolio pioneers. These problems were so overwhelming that pursuing a model of school-wide participation became inevitable. In this model, all staff are encouraged to participate and every effort must be made to provide support to everyone. There can be many choices about the style and degree of faculty participation, but everyone should be expected to join in the effort in their own way.

Everyone is affected when there are changes in curriculum and assessment within a school. In changing from a closed- to open-door culture, everyone is invited and encouraged to be part of the conversation surrounding those changes. Each person does not have to agree with or like what others are doing but everyone should engage with the community openly and respectfully. Disagreements and different perspectives should be discussed.

3. Learn about Teaching and Learning from Looking at Student Work

Looking at and talking about student work is a center-piece of these practices. Why? We believe that the things children make in school are unique expressions of their hands and minds at work. Through careful and nonjudgmental examination and discussion of these works, we can explore what the child is interested in, trying to create, and aiming to communicate. Through consideration of the assignment and the materials and resources used, we can see the kind of learning environment in which the child was working.

By looking at both the child and the learning environment, we can begin to raise questions about how children learn and how schools can support, encourage, and challenge that process. The purpose of these conversations is to provide a structured setting in which faculty and staff regularly sit and learn together from thoughtful consideration of student work. These settings provide an opportunity for staff to learn from each other as they listen to and consider the diverse perspectives expressed by the group. Many of these sessions raise more questions than they answer. That's fine if they cause those participating to stop, note, and wonder about the complexity and seriousness of children's work.

HOW REFLECTIVE PRACTICES HELP PORTFOLIOS TAKE ROOT IN A SCHOOL

When we began to examine the conditions and forces in schools that operate against the implementation of portfolio assessment, we knew that isolation was a critical factor. We also recognized that teachers needed some immediate or quick satisfaction from the work required by portfolios. In some cases, the assessment activities teachers tried were instantly rewarding. Children responded with such honesty and delight to the opportunity to write reflections, for example, that their teachers were sold overnight on the value of the effort. In other cases—even with the very same kinds of activities—the results were far less satisfying.

Why did essentially the same activity work take hold so quickly in one classroom and not nearly as well or as quickly in another? There were too many variables to be certain about the conditions for quick success. Through observation and a lot of talking with teachers and students, it became clear that perseverance was key to eventual success. It wasn't simply doing the same activity over and over that did the trick. It was keen observation, conversations with students and thorough analysis of their work that slowly but surely guided teachers toward alterations and adjustments in their approach to the activity, and ultimately to success. Reflection is quite a new form of thinking and writing for many students. Collecting and selecting work for a portfolio can seem silly to children who have only seen their work discarded or ignored once it has been graded.

If quick satisfaction isn't guaranteed, we reasoned, something else would have to happen to keep teachers engaged in portfolio work. Building reflective practice into the life of the school serves this purpose. Teachers can share small successes and big frustrations. They can encourage each other when individually they would simply choose to go back to what is familiar. They are reminded with each session that others are involved in the same effort. Each teacher may be focusing her portfolio work in particular ways; but in schools where the whole staff is involved, there is great comfort and encouragement in knowing that everyone is working toward the same goal.

WHAT'S NEW HERE

Any educator reading this book will recognize that these portfolio practices comprise aspects of professional activities that have been used in schools for years. Elements of teacher research, quality management, teamwork and teacher collaboration, a strong focus on student work, a conscious blending of theory and practice and community involvement lace through these practices. But, like portfolios themselves, these practices highlight the products of students' and teachers' work and they require time for thoughtful and collaborative reflection.

The ingredients we suggest are not new, but are put together specifically to respond to the challenges of portfolio assessment. Through our research we observed firsthand many of the challenges of and obstacles to implementing the use of portfolios in schools. The practices discussed in this book have emerged from collaborative efforts with many practitioners. We have mixed many of the most effective professional practices in current use, applied them specifically to a portfolio-focused context, and experimented with various structures and activities. The results are these portfolio practices.

IN THIS BOOK YOU WILL FIND...

Part One: Collecting Student Work

Chapter 1, **Designing a Portfolio System,** examines many of the questions to be considered in developing an approach to creating portfolios. What do portfolios look like? How do they work in different classrooms? What are the purposes in keeping them? What are some things that must be kept in mind while developing a process of portfolio assessment?

Part Two: Portfolio Practices Within the Classroom

The two practices in Part Two take place in the classroom of an individual teacher or in conversations among a teacher and colleagues. In this research we learned that portfolio assessment, when done properly, can become an integral part of classroom life and of each teacher's practice.

Chapter 2, **Experimenting in the Classroom,** talks about how to design and carry out small-scale "experiments" in the classroom. The idea here is to try something new on a small, manageable scale to find out if it works before making lots of changes.

Chapter 3, **Collaborative Assessment: Examining and Evaluating Student Work,** suggests ideas for structuring conversations among teachers in a collaborative spirit around collections of student work.

Part Three: Portfolio Practices Across Classrooms

Part Three makes a transition to practices that affect school-wide policy and structure. Without the involvement of the entire school, portfolio practices will not take root. No significant educational practice can be sustained unless it is firmly embedded in the culture of the school: teachers need to be supported to take time to try out things; students must learn to participate in setting goals, recognizing accomplishments and evaluating their progress; and parents will begin to rely on—and appreciate—the information they get from assessments based on collections of their children's work.

Chapter 4, **Sharing Language and Ideas,** focuses on building a common language and theory of learning—a very important element of the school-wide portfolio culture. We talk about why this language is a prerequisite as well as a logical outcome of a school-wide portfolio system.

Chapter 5, **Bi-focal Assessment,** suggests how portfolios can be used to assess the educational program as well as the students' learning. Reading portfolios must always be "bi-focal" in its analysis, shifting constantly from focus on the individual student to looking more broadly at the program itself.

Chapter 6, **Protecting and Sustaining Innovation,** explores steps that teachers can take to ensure that their innovative assessment practices are protected from the various influences that can stifle productive change.

Part Four: Before the Practices

Chapter 7, **Portfolio Research at Project Zero,** recounts our work addressing portfolio practices with teachers and schools over the course of two major research projects. Our research with these teachers and schools gave us the chance to observe, document and report their experiences in some detail, but it also allowed us to interact with them, to make suggestions, and to help them further their work. The experiences of these teachers gave us a rich and convincing context for making more general claims.

HOW TO READ THIS BOOK

First, Don't Read This Book Alone!

We believe that portfolio practice is most powerful when it is a collaborative effort, undertaken by groups of teachers and even whole schools. The same applies to reading the book. Find a partner or form a study group and talk over the points that are raised.

You may find allies more quickly than you think. Most professional organizations are paying careful attention to alternative forms of assessment and their journals currently reflect that attention. So even if you don't read with a partner and you don't foresee dramatic changes in assessment practices in your school or district, you will find a great deal of conversation about these issues outside the school.

Second, Hang in There!

Over the course of eight years of research on portfolio assessment, we have watched the term "portfolio" evolve from esoterica in the arts to the urgency of a buzzword. While this has created an audience for this research, that interest often carries unrealistic expectations along with it. Everything we describe in this book can be done in regular classrooms, but most of it cannot be done quickly or even easily.

As you read, remember that this work requires patience, diligence, and understanding. The practices we describe challenge many of the basic assumptions of contemporary educational practice. We believe that the challenge can be met successfully by all teachers, but only if they give themselves enough time and receive the necessary support.

Part One

COLLECTING STUDENT WORK

Portfolios are not new. They have been used in the art world for some time as well as in certain educational settings. Teachers need to develop a design for portfolios and an approach to using them in the classroom that grows directly out of their needs and concerns. Chapter 1, **Designing a Portfolio System**, discusses critical issues in the process of developing an approach to portfolio assessment and makes concrete suggestions about what that process might look like.

Chapter 1

DESIGNING A PORTFOLIO SYSTEM

Portfolios are thoughtful collections of student work meant for active and often long-term review. To design a system of portfolio assessment, each teacher must decide what to collect. That simple decision leads to the consideration of the purpose, the audience and the use of those portfolios.

Portfolio assessment is based on two very simple ideas—that students can demonstrate what they are learning and what they understand through organized collections of their work, and that their learning can be assessed through those collections. Because portfolios are tangible and substantial, teachers always ask "What do they look like and how do they work?" In this chapter, we address these questions.

Designing portfolio assessment for a classroom or a school is very much like building a bridge. All bridges have certain properties in common and they must all obey certain laws of physics; but each is unique as well. Bridge builders dedicate considerable effort in surveying the site, measuring the relevant environmental conditions, determining the demands of use, and assessing the resources and materials that are available for construction. In much the same way, all portfolio systems have certain properties in common and must obey the "laws" of learning. At the same time, each system must attend to the needs, resources, and interests of one's locality.

Using sample portfolios, this chapter describes the four essential elements of portfolio design—contents, time frame, structure, and student involvement. It describes portfolios in the day-to-day flow of activities in the classroom and outlines key considerations of portfolio practice such as the purpose and audience. Finally, we describe four very different kinds of portfolio systems that can emerge from various elements and considerations.

THE ELEMENTS OF PORTFOLIOS

The four essential elements of all portfolio systems are: 1) contents, the actual collections of student work; 2) time frame, the period of time covered; 3) structure or organizing principles; and 4) student involvement.

Contents of Portfolios

A portfolio is the collection of artifacts produced by students during the course of their studies. These artifacts can include written pieces, reports, performances, maps, experiments, and community services. The goal of any portfolio system is to demonstrate, through these archives of their work, what students have learned and understood .

The draft of a short story or the final version of a term paper are typical things that might be included in a portfolio. Writing almost always yields tangible and lasting documents that are easily archived. Other kinds of student work do not yield the same kinds of evidence.

For instance, in producing a play, the final performance is tangible evidence for evaluation, but other important elements of the production, such as collaborative work or "behind the scenes" preparations, may not leave a trace that can be easily judged. In such cases, the student might document her efforts with videotape or journal accounts in the portfolio. Similarly, a portfolio project in robotics lab, or an internship in a community center would require special effort to document the work that is momentary and elusive.

A portfolio might include an examination or a standardized test—if it showed learning. In each case, however, *the work archived in the portfolio must demonstrate some form of understanding.* This is what distinguishes the portfolio from the complete collections of exercises of the work folder or lab notebook.

Here are possible tables of contents from two different portfolios. A social studies portfolio might include these materials:

- written materials—drafts, notes, logs
- videotape records—presentations, performances, or conversations
- photographs—interim stages, a final record of product
- audio tape records—performances, readings
- maps, drawings, sketches, paintings
- measures of achievement—test scores, performance records

A writing portfolio, in contrast, might include:

- a satisfying, high quality piece
- a less-than-satisfying, lower quality piece
- a "free pick" selected by the student
- a "free pick" selected by the teacher
- student reflections on each major piece
- student logs or journal entries that provide a picture of the development of insight and working process (the choices and discoveries they make, their concerns, resources, frustrations)
- at least one "biography of a work" that includes all notes, drafts, revisions and reflections that contributed to the completion of the project

The Time Frame

Learning always takes a sustained effort. An important difference between portfolios and examinations is that a portfolio system can capture efforts over a relatively extended period. In creating a portfolio system, teachers acknowledge the complexity of students' undertakings and the importance of their perseverance.

Looking at work over an extended period provides the opportunity for students to undertake more complex tasks. Assessment that is focused on quick right answers tends to stifle risk-taking, experimentation, or challenge. In contrast, a portfolio system provides a setting that allows for error, failed attempts, and dead ends. It looks over longer periods for corrections of errors, solutions to problems, and productive or creative changes in direction. All of these are attributes of complex problem-solving and all require an extended view.

To illustrate progress, risks, and invention, portfolios must contain more than the finished piece or final performance; they should reflect steps along the way.

A table of contents for a science project portfolio might include:

- brainstorming notes that led to the project concept
- the work plan that the student followed as a time-line
- student log that records successes and difficulties
- review of the actual research and results
- photograph of the finished project
- student reflections on the overall experience

In the above example, components such as the student log and the work plan can capture some aspects of the student's progress over the course of a unit. Although the portfolio contents do not show the processes of creating the project, analysis by students and teachers illustrate how the project evolved.

The Structure

Like any meaningful collection, a portfolio must be carefully organized. Organization distinguishes the portfolio from a work folder, lab notebook or writing journal, and establishes the intention of the portfolio. It also makes the portfolio easier to interpret and analyze.

Organizing elements of a mathematics portfolio might include:

- a table of contents
- an introduction or title page that identifies the student and explains what can be found in the collection, and the purpose of the portfolio
- brief descriptions of selected assignments for readers less familiar with the operation of the classroom
- labels that distinguish attempted solutions from the final report
- dates on all entries
- a review section that includes student reflections and self-assessments, together with teacher comments and peer comments that can help provide important information about the expectations, standards and critical atmosphere in which the various projects were produced.

Student Involvement

Portfolio assessment provides a unique opportunity for students to become involved in their own assessment in several ways.

First, the students are involved with their teachers in selecting the work that will be included. Involving students in selection gives them a sense of ownership of the portfolio; it also gives them a new purpose for completing their assignments.

Second, students are drawn into the process of assessing or evaluating the work in their portfolios. This involvement can happen as peer critique in a process writing class, as brainstorming criteria of excellence for a social studies project, or as meeting with the teacher over the quality of a given piece. In each case, the discussion considers why a piece is successful, or not, and what might be done differently to improve it.

Third, students can comment on their learning and their achievements through systematic reflection exercises. Through their experiences selecting and critiquing the work, students can review their progress, describe what issues they tackled and plan their next attempts. These reflections are important because they give students a voice in defining their work; the reflections are important to the teacher because they often yield invaluable insight into the students' perspective on their learning.

THE PORTFOLIO SYSTEM IN THE CLASSROOM

The previous elements of portfolios give a sense of what these documents look like. However, designing a portfolio system for the classroom is very individualized because it depends on your teaching style, the needs of your school, and the expectations of your community. Nevertheless, every portfolio system involves three basic activities: 1) collecting and organizing that work; 2) reviewing work; and 3) reporting the results.

Collecting and Organizing the Work

The selection of portfolio work is usually conducted jointly by the students and teacher. (Some teachers, however, make the selections themselves and others turn the entire decision over to the students.) The advantage of the joint approach is that it gives the students a sense of ownership while allowing the teacher to maintain some control over the contents. As the portfolios grow in size during the year, the teacher might ask the students periodically to remove pieces. Many teachers also write their own comments on the student work and these are also added to the portfolio collection as well.

The major difference between a portfolio and a work folder is in organization. In the portfolio, each piece has been selected for a reason and those reasons are recorded as part of the collection. Entries also are dated so that later review of the portfolio allows the reader to see the changes in student performance over time. The portfolio also often includes a narrative thread that ties the components together.

The portfolio can be further organized with structural elements such as a table of contents, explanations of assignments, or background on the class. Once a routine has been established students will collect and organize their work fairly efficiently, without taking a lot of class time. Even young children can work cooperatively, checking one anothers' work to ensure that the collections are complete and well organized.

Reviewing the Work

Each portfolio is an active document. As the year progresses pieces are constantly added and removed. These changes must be thoughtful and documented. Another aspect of this review is to gain perspective on the developing skills in the students; this is how portfolio assessment is used for improvement.

In reviewing the portfolio, students record their observations and recommendations for future efforts. These thoughts are part of the portfolio and become an important organizing and reviewing element. Reflection also underscores the student's own role in creating the portfolio, just as it reflects the student's role in creating the work.

Some teachers create special reflection exercises in which students work in pairs to review their portfolios, record what they learn, then add those written pieces to the work itself. Often this review also includes the selection of new pieces and removal of older ones. In each case, the students record their choices, their reactions, and their thoughts. Later, the teacher can review these reflections with the student or with the student and parents or with colleagues.

Students and teacher together review portfolios for evidence of understanding and or improvements in skills. In making these determinations, students make important judgments of their work and of themselves. These reviews occur periodically (perhaps once each quarter). Portfolio review should not be conducted at the very end of the year. Regular review keeps the portfolios and the judgments very much on the minds of all students as they approach each assignment. A kindergarten teacher told us that she knew portfolios had taken hold in her class when she heard one student say to another at the easel, "You're not going to put that in your portfolio, are you?"

All assessment ultimately boils down to a question of judgment. In the professions, assessment is often the judgment of one professional by another, but it can also be the self-critical judgment of one's own work. From medicine to sculpture to woodworking, assessment requires constant judgment. Participants in these fields must persistently strive to improve their ability to make those judgments properly. The mere existence of portfolios in a classroom does not mean that there has been any assessment. To assess them means that someone (teacher or student) has read everything in the portfolio and then made judgments about the quality of what has been read.

Reporting the Results

Perhaps the most challenging aspect of portfolio assessment is the task of reporting the results. Part of the difficulty is the natural inclination to think in terms of grades, percentiles or ranks, which are efficient, familiar, easily communicated, and relatively well understood. Portfolios can be reported in the same way; they can be graded like lab reports or ranked like science fair projects.

But, the shortcomings of these reduced forms of reporting are obvious. A rich collection of a student's work, when that work is challenging and ranges over a variety of topics, will have many different features. To encapsulate a careful reading of the work in the grade "B+" misses much of the point.

An alternative is the narrative report, a more detailed synopsis and analysis of the portfolio. Some schools use written narratives instead of grades in their traditional report cards. The narrative report also can be shared verbally in parent conferences or in faculty meetings. The teacher and the parent or other teachers go through the portfolio together, talking over what they find.

The point is that grades are not the assessment; they are a technique used to report the outcome of an assessment. The act of making the judgment or assigning the grade is the actual assessment. Portfolio assessment and grading systems are not mutually exclusive. Portfolios can be graded and reported, but portfolio assessment offers much more than can be captured meaningfully in a single grade or set of grades.

CONSIDERATIONS IN THE DESIGN OF A PORTFOLIO SYSTEM

Designing a system of portfolio assessment involves making choices. Four elements to consider are: 1) purpose; 2) audience; 3) range of work; and 4) presentation.

The Purpose

The general purpose of all systems of portfolio assessment is to demonstrate what students have learned and what they understand. Beyond that, however, you must think about identifying purposes more specifically. You could target student interests in particular; you could focus on demonstration of specific skills within a discipline; you could record students' grasp and use of essential information; you could document facility at communicating what they had learned, and so on.

Those are very different purposes and the design of the portfolio system should reflect them. Another aspect of the assessment system is how it will be used. One portfolio system might be used to hold students accountable for their work; a very different system would report individual differences to parents; a third might be used to evaluate the educational system.

The decisions related to purpose ultimately reflect the educational values of the teacher, the school or district. We have found that the act of designing a portfolio system reveals these values often for the first time. Conversely, changing a school's system of assessment is often difficult, not because of the professed educational purposes of the school, but because the true purposes are quite different.

Here is an example: A middle school states that its mission is to educate all its students to their highest ability and that it focuses on emerging competence and individual proclivities. However, when the school evaluates its students, it uses examinations that compare the performance of the individual to the performance of the group rather than assessments that compare performance with that student's performances in the past. Indeed, the true purpose of the school's assessment is not to meet the stated mission, but to screen students into ability groups in the high school. Attempting to change the assessment system in such a school may be extremely difficult because changes will raise many unexpected questions.

The Audience

There are as many different purposes for an assessment system as there are different audiences. To see the impact of audience, imagine that you have installed a portfolio system and near the end of the year you are ready to report the results. To whom are you reporting? Who cares how your students are doing?

In every school there are many constituents, each of whom is a potential audience for the results of the portfolio assessment system:

- the parents of individual students
- the department of testing and evaluation in the central office
- the school committee
- next year's teachers for each student
- your colleagues in your department
- a community group concerned with property values
- your students
- employers for whom students are job candidates
- college admissions offices

These audiences are often interested in different qualities of the educational experience in your classroom or school. A portfolio system designed for one audience may be very difficult for others to interpret. Different audiences demand different forms of evidence as demonstration of learning.

The students themselves are an audience for portfolios and many portfolio systems deal with this by investing the students with a sense of ownership. Some teachers feel quite strongly that it is essential for students to be centrally involved in deciding what should go into their portfolios. Student ownership and involvement is the point of portfolio use for these teachers. They see students' active participation in crafting this picture of their work and the sense of perspective and, often, pride that comes from presenting their portfolio as a central goal of the whole endeavor.

The Range of Work

Since the focus of any portfolio system is on the work that students do, the design must carefully consider what kind of work will be included. What is the focus of study in a given classroom? What subjects, skills, behaviors, attitudes, etc. are students and teachers working on? What are the specific artifacts that students produce and which can be meaningfully saved in a portfolio?

The portfolio system might consider a range of quality in the work included. For instance, if rough drafts and early efforts are included, then these can be compared with later drafts and more sophisticated efforts. The work spans a developmental range; across that range, it can demonstrate growth and learning. Other portfolio systems might expressly reduce the range of work by concentrating exclusively on finished pieces.

In addition, the portfolio system might expand the range of work by including aspects of students' efforts that are outside of the skills and concepts under study in the classroom. Personal interests or individual strengths can be demonstrated in a portfolio; aptitudes for empathy and interpersonal communication might be captured. Some portfolio systems deem such student attributes as relevant, but in others, they are not.

Presentation

In any portfolio system, the portfolios themselves are substantial entities. They can be cumbersome to store and difficult to handle. They may require special equipment. In designing your system, always keep in mind the issue of display.

Some of these issues are as simple as finding the right folders or storage containers. Others are more conceptual, such as providing appropriate background material to make the portfolios readable by someone less familiar with the classroom. Still other issues are aesthetic: Does the portfolio capture the true effort or intention of the student?

These presentational issues can be important to both the reader and to the student. The portfolios are not only a collection of the student's work, they are also reflections of the student's efforts and intentions. Simultaneously, the portfolios reflect the concerns of the teacher, and the resources that are available.

At the same time, however, it may be tempting to create a process that becomes unwieldy or impractical in the day-to-day classroom. Too many examples often are less revealing than fewer, carefully chosen examples. To prevent this, the realities of the classroom as well as availability of resources must be kept firmly in mind. For example, photographs often are a quick way of recording events, but they can be costly in terms of processing and they can take time away from other activities. Photocopying can produce duplicates cheaply but often with a loss of resolution or color. Video materials provide rich records but they are extremely difficult to organize and time-consuming to review. Storage and retrieval are issues that have to be considered.

DIFFERENT FORMS OF PORTFOLIO DESIGNS

Because portfolio systems must be designed to address specific audiences, to achieve very specific assessment purposes, and to evaluate a wide range of student efforts, they take on very different forms. These various forms are distinct and the portfolios in one form are not necessarily comparable to those in another.

This section illustrates these differences with four examples of portfolio designs.

1. Cross-discipline Portfolios

Portfolios of this type are collections of work from across various subject areas and made over the course of a term or the year. Many elementary school portfolios are in this category. There is usually a tremendous range of work—writing in many genres, art work, project materials, models, documentation of performances, reports, experiments and so on. This diversity reflects the variety of activities, subjects under study and skills being practiced in the classroom. The work collected represent s drafts or stages of production as well as final products.

If you want your assessment to capture the student as a whole, then the portfolio system should have a cross-disciplinary aspect. This type of portfolio is especially effective at capturing developmental changes, and at showing children's interests or questions. The challenge is to prevent cross-discipline efforts from becoming unstructured collections that lack purpose.

For example, a portfolio system developed for a fourth-grade classroom might develop a composite profile of the strengths and preferences of each student in the class. Or high school students applying for community internships might develop portfolios that demonstrate well-rounded skills in a variety of prescribed disciplines.

2. Discipline-based Portfolios

These portfolios document skills or accomplishments valued in a specific discipline such as writing, visual arts, social studies, or mathematics. A typical example of this type of portfolio is created in a writing workshop, sometimes called "workshop portfolios." The collection of work is focused on one discipline—writing—and sometimes only one genre of writing: poetry, for example. The focus is quite specific and allows for the creation of an in-depth picture of a student's work in this one area.

The specific focus of these portfolios makes it easy to use them to chart the up-and-down paths of growth and development in a discipline, and not see it only in retrospect.

The similarity of the various pieces of work facilitates comparisons between works that are often difficult in more diverse works.

Discipline-based portfolios are more focused for both teacher and students. The portfolio created in a writing workshop by middle school students has a distinct purpose and identity for them. One teacher said, "Their portfolios are really useful to them all along, not just at the end of the year. They carry them around and want to show them to everyone." In high school, a portfolio structured around a continuing set of experiments in biology class would have the same focus on a particular discipline.

3. Pass-along Portfolios

Portfolios that are passed along to the student's teachers the following year must be treated as a separate category. This type of portfolio serves as an introduction, providing continuity from one year to the next and communication among the grades. This portfolio type can be used also to create a multi-year, cross-grade view of a child's development. Such a record is invaluable for teachers in situations where there is concern over a child's progress. A cumulative record of work encourages looking at the continuum of a child's growth and learning rather than viewing development in relation to grade-specific markers.

We found very few schools in which pass-along portfolios were used effectively for these purposes. Many teachers talked instead about having their own methods of diagnosing new students skills. Some said that they prefer to meet the children and get to know them in person before seeing their previous work or reading another teacher's assessment of them. Unfortunately, this lack of enthusiasm suggests that school organization encourages teachers to think of themselves as teachers of a certain age child or of a certain subject rather than as individuals closely involved with others in the multi-year education of children.

In one school, however, the student and teacher choose a small sample of work from the portfolio at the end of the year while the bulk of the work in the portfolio goes home in June. The selected pieces are then added, year after year, to the growing collection. No more than about ten pieces of work are saved each year along with some photos and student reflections.

4. Graduation Portfolios

Graduation portfolios demonstrate the levels of mastery and creativity achieved by students during their school years, but they reflect much less of the educational process. High school seniors might use these portfolios in applying to college or in job interviews. In such cases, presentation of material is a critical element of the portfolio.

We know of only a few high schools currently using—or planning to use—graduation portfolios. At the Rindge School of Technical Arts in Cambridge, Massachusetts, the staff is beginning to explore the use of portfolios as part of students' application processes to apprenticeship programs the school has established with local colleges, businesses and hospitals. This use of portfolios will become the model for the kind of portfolios the staff wants student to have after four years—an impressive, comprehensive collection of both academic work and work in the trades. In time, as colleges and employers indicate that they want to see the work their applicants have already completed as a way to measure desirability and appropriateness for their programs, graduation portfolios will become a more commonplace feature of high school life.

LOOKING AHEAD

Because portfolio assessment can do so many things and address so many different audiences, it may be tempting to try to do all of them and address everyone. This is unwise. Trying to do everything for everyone simply begs many of the questions and considerations we have outlined. If your audience is "everyone," then it really is no one. If you try to do everything with a single portfolio, you will not do any of it very well.

Instead, take each of our considerations carefully to heart and make precise decisions about each one. Once you have decided on an audience and a purpose stick to it; don't try to adapt your system to someone or something else. Don't try to satisfy the other audiences.

Throughout the design, keep in mind your audience. Portfolios are meant to be read, so make them readable. Don't assume that the reader has detailed knowledge of the child, the classroom, or the school. The work must be displayed in a presentable form if it is to be taken seriously. Include enough student work in the design to create a rich picture, but not more than is needed. It is better to create a focused portfolio around a selected set of issues or questions than to collect a little bit of a lot of things.

Think about the type of portfolio you settle on. Will it focus on a discipline, on the child, on graduation? Don't try to make the portfolio do something for which it was not designed.

You now should have a sense of what a portfolio system might look like in your classroom and how it might be used on a day-to-day basis. In the next section, we talk about the various activities, or practices, that you can undertake as you design and implement a system of portfolio assessment in your classroom.

Part Two

PORTFOLIO PRACTICES WITHIN THE CLASSROOM

In Part Two, we describe two portfolio practices that are centered in classrooms. They involve teachers in considering classroom instruction and assessment and the work children create in school. Through these practices, teachers identify questions they want to investigate, plan experiments that will provide answers to these questions and carefully study the resulting work

We devote a chapter to each of these practices. Chapter 2, **Experimenting in the Classroom**, explores the design and implementation of modest changes in assessment practices. Chapter 3, **Collaborative Assessment**, shows how to work with colleagues to examine student work carefully and how, from that examination, to raise questions about student learning.

Chapter 2

EXPERIMENTING IN THE CLASSROOM

Designing and refining new assessment activities is part of the ongoing, year-after-year work of developing and sustaining vital assessment practices. Constant experimentation assures the school community that its assessments are responsive to the changing needs of teachers, children, parents and administrators.

THESE QUESTIONS HAVE BEEN ON YOUR MIND

You have twenty-three third-graders. Writing is a major activity in your classroom. Children are writing every day—letters, daily reports on the eating habits of Jake (the garden snake who lives in the science corner), short articles for the two-page weekly paper on newsworthy school events that goes home every Friday, book reviews, poems, and many other forms of written communication. You love reading children's writing. You believe that regular, frequent writing in a variety of genres is good for their development. But you often wonder if you are really providing the kind of response and feedback that helps students become better writers.

You have noticed that most of your students have definite opinions about the quality of the individual pieces they write. Sometimes they are pleased and proud and other times they would be happy to leave their work on the bus—and they do! To make matters more complicated, sometimes you agree with them, but other times you have a very different assessment of their work. How do such young writers have such strong opinions of their work? Where do these opinions come from? You wonder about their standards and criteria for good writing and how to explain the discrepancy between their perspectives and yours.

These questions have been on your mind for some time but you've never had the opportunity to pursue them in any structured way. Fortunately, your staff has been reconsidering their assessment practices and you've been encouraged to identify aspects of children's learning experiences in your classroom that you need to understand in greater depth in order to improve your teaching. You chose this issue. But what in the world will you do to investigate it?

SUSIE HANLEY, KINDERGARTEN TEACHER

At first, it was a curiosity of my own. I was at a point where I was thinking that portfolios were interesting and I was creating the kind of data I wanted. In a way, I was very teacher-directed in that there were only a few opportunities where the kids really got to be in their portfolios and use their portfolios. I wondered, "Was I asking them for feedback at all. My attempts to get where I am now have been focused around how I can make the portfolio an everyday thing. I knew that I needed to embed more active portfolio time within the classroom so I experimented with making it a regular part of what we were doing all the time in order to really transfer the ownership of the portfolios.

At the beginning of building portfolios with children in the classroom, I was very wide open and impressionable in terms of what kinds of things we could collect and how articulate a kindergarten child can become in terms of her process about doing the work and reflecting on the work. In my attempt to try and find a starting spot, I started having them pull out what I thought were their best pieces, and from that came an experiment with building criteria: for example, I would say to them, "You're about to do a task; what are the criteria for doing a good writing piece?" That was a first step, in terms of trying to talk about why a piece of work was their best piece. From that we went on to other ways in which we could pull out work or sort and look at the work, making additional opportunities for them to use their portfolio as a learning tool about themselves, and about them as a worker.

I soon suggested that they try pulling their portfolios apart and sorting the contents by disciplines. This was an extension of choosing their best work. I wanted them to see that a scientist had to use numbers and had to write, that tasks you are asked to do are not strictly one kind of work or another. That's what the sorting turned out to be; that is, sitting closely with each child and listening to him deliberate out loud most times: "Gee, this is science work, but I also did writing; I could put it in the art pile because I did some great drawings in my observation booklet." I was listening to them try to make that decision, for ways in which they understood some of the things that I had modeled or put out there as ways in which work connects across disciplines.

THE PRACTICE OF EXPERIMENTING WITH ASSESSMENTS IN THE CLASSROOM

We see experimenting with assessments in the classroom as both a way of starting work with portfolios and a way of ensuring that portfolio assessment develops, evolves and remains vital and useful for students and teachers over years. Through our research, we've identified some common aspects of portfolio work many teachers have explored through their classroom experiments. While not an exhaustive list, it does identify some of the major problems and issues teachers tackle in implementing portfolio assessment. We have seen many experiments in documentation, collection and selection, working with the language of assessment, reflection and reporting.

Developing assessment experiments to try in a classroom depends first and foremost on having something you want to learn about your students and then on your creativity in designing ways to find answers to your questions. Once tried in the classroom, the experiments are not complete until there has been a careful study of the results. Several principles have emerged as useful in guiding this practice: 1) start small; 2) study what happens carefully; and 3) build in support and review.

Start Small

There are two basic approaches to changing assessment practices in the classroom. The first argues that the old ways don't work, should be thrown out and replaced with something new—A.S.A.P.! The other approach sees this process much like redesigning a boat while it is out on the high seas. If you start ripping up the floor boards too quickly without having taken some care in designing both the new model and the process of transition, you probably will find yourself sinking—fast. At that point, most of us would do the same thing: conclude that the new model isn't working and start throwing the floor boards back where they used to be.

The frame of the new boat should be as well constructed as possible before the old frame is discarded. Care, thoughtfulness, an evolving sense of why these changes are being made and what students will gain from them are crucial to the initiative's success. In schools where the staff or individual teachers have "gone portfolio" overnight, the portfolios often end up lost, forgotten or on the shelf. New practices must, bit by bit, prove their value to everyone involved (teachers, children, parents, administrators). Starting small is a key to that process.

Small, in this case, refers to the scale and scope of the experiment. In a classroom where problem-solving is highly valued and much of the school day is structured around creating opportunities for seeking solutions to real questions, assessing the effect of those activities is critical. By experimenting with the focused question, "Are my students really growing as problem-solvers?", the teacher will learn many practical lessons about designing and conducting elements of portfolio assessment. She also will learn a lot about her students and their experience in her classroom.

Another reason to start small is to make the risks more manageable. After all, experimenting means trying something out for the first time. Success is not guaranteed. Keeping the stakes low helps to create an atmosphere of true experimentation. Things may not work. Often they don't the first time. There is no shame in this. It is an honorable part of conducting experiments. Even unsuccessful experiments have important lessons for us—if we look carefully at the reasons for the failure.

Three years later, Susie recalls her first experiments with portfolios in her kindergarten classroom.

SUSIE HANLEY, KINDERGARTEN TEACHER

My experiments changed and grew over time. There are probably now about ten different activities that I do with portfolio review. I still have them sort out their best work, but I try for a real exploration of "why." For example, "why is this your best piece, and why do you think it's good?" Some of that happens in a class group or small group context, and some happens in a personal conference with the child, the portfolio, and myself. Another activity I do at this point is called "red and green." The children are given pieces of red construction paper and green construction paper and sort through their portfolios, placing the things that they think are excellent examples of their work on the green paper, signaling that it should "keep going" in the portfolio. Things they put on the red paper are things that are no longer their best work, no longer please them, no longer considered quality pieces, etc.

After "red and green," which they do a number of times, a child will trade portfolios with a friend and look through it, pulling aside and pointing out what they think are the best pieces and why they are good. Later in the year they do a "red, yellow and green": green is "keep going", red is "stop, get it out of there!" and yellow is "not quite in the best pile yet," because it might need more practice, a brand new skill that hasn't been mastered, or needs more time and opportunity to work on it so that it can be moved out of yellow and into green.

So now my kids are producing something in the classroom and they are asking questions such as: "can I run to the office to get a Xerox of this so that I can take it home and put the original in my portfolio? Is this something we take home today or is this something that's going into the portfolio? My best example of my writing is in my portfolio, can I go and get it?" It's really their collection and I'm helping them develop the language of looking at their work, setting goals for themselves about what they need to do next. I think I'm modeling a lot of that language and setting the expectation that we are always working towards best work and reminding them of the agreed-upon qualities that we have talked about for good work. For example, in my one-on-one conferences with a student, I might say, "Here's all your work. What do you think we could work on in terms of writing? What do you think might be another thing you could concentrate on?"

Study Carefully What Happens

The experiment is not over once the classroom activity has been tried. To paraphrase Plato's famous line about life, *The experiment which is unexamined is not worth conducting*. In the examining, we make sense of what has happened and of lessons that are learned. Studying what happens in the course of these experiments is actually part and parcel of assessing portfolios. The focus is not restricted to questions about the progress of individual children. It is, rather, on the question that guided the experiment, the activities tried in the classroom and students' responses. Borrowing ideas from the assessment of portfolios provides some useful clues to the examination of these experiments. The first idea is to look carefully at what students produce.

We found that teachers based their evaluation of the success of an experiment on impressions and little more. A teacher's gut feelings are crucial indicators but they are not the whole story. Often, teachers hardly read what students wrote or made notes on what they said before they decided that the experiment was a success or failure.

If you ask students to write reflections, for example, and you want to know if those reflections can provide specific ideas about how to help students progress, then read what they've written. Read them once and then read them again after a day or two or more. Look at the reflections in relation to the work being discussed. Look at them in relation to each other, that is, one student's to another's. Look for patterns and categories in the reflections. The categories can be determined from your reading of the reflections. Emotions, for example, may be a way to categorize them. Frustration, pride, confusion, delight or any other emotions may be expressed in the reflections. Looking for patterns in who, when and in relation to what can reveal a great deal about how students feel about their work—and why.

These same reflections can also be categorized according to things students feel they need to work on. These same reflections might be placed on a continuum for level of detail and specificity students used in discussing their work. The categories or continuums you establish should add to the information needed to answer questions addressed by the experiments.

Similarly, if your experiment involves encouraging students to select pieces for their portfolios, look at what they select. Try to understand their choices. Think about these choices in relation to other things you know about this group and specific children in the group. Often the choices they make reveal their sense of what portfolios are for as well as their perceptions of themselves and what they think of as work worth saving and presenting. We met a middle school student who did humorous work—cartoons, funny stories, dialogues for comedy sketches—but never chose any of this work for his portfolio. His teacher really enjoyed his sense of humor and asked why he hadn't included any of this funny material. He was reluctant to do that, he explained, because he thought his portfolio was supposed to be his serious work. It hadn't really occurred to him, until his teacher suggested otherwise, that he was quite serious about his humor, that he put great effort into making it work and that it was a source of pride for him.

In addition to looking carefully at what students produce, it can be extremely helpful to make notes on what children say and do when engaged in a new activity. Making notes provides a way to structure recall. So many things happen in a single minute in a classroom that it is impossible to remember all of them. Sitting down to jot bits of conversation or observations of behaviors and actions can actually bring back far more than one might otherwise remember. The more details captured, the richer the picture to work with in analyzing what the experience was like for students.

Finally, it can be extremely helpful to share your "data" with colleagues. Outsiders, as we note over and over in discussing these practices, can see things in a classroom that the teacher simply doesn't see, or sees but doesn't name. Pursuing any way of seeing more than one normally sees is worth the effort.

Build In Support and Review

No matter how experienced a teacher is, everyone trying new forms of assessment in the classroom needs support and the perspective of colleagues. The partners or small groups that formed for reflective analysis can naturally continue to consider the effectiveness of your classroom experiments. Even if these groups do not meet frequently, they should meet regularly. Once a month is a good idea and four times a year a minimum if the group is to be useful to the participants. Keeping the groups small makes it easier to arrange meetings, but administrative support is critical to establish and protect the time needed for these conversations.

The focus of these conversations, once experiments are underway, is on ways of judging the effectiveness of the new activities. Teachers must come to these meetings prepared to remind others (and themselves) why they undertook their experiments in the first place. Then they have to describe what they actually have done in the classroom and how it went, including students' responses and any writing or sample collections made by students. Finally, they must discuss their own assessment of the experience. The other teachers, in turn, respond with questions and interpretations of this "data."

Frequently we found that teachers had decided that their portfolio activities were "not working" or were "too much trouble." When we looked carefully at what they had done and the evidence on which they based these conclusions, we often disagreed. In some cases, relatively simple alterations made the portfolio experiment much more successful. In other cases, a fresh perspective on student responses revealed much more thought and engagement from students than was initially evident to the teacher.

This discrepancy surprised us. Even though we were collaborating with experienced and innovative teachers, we found that they were often disappointed and even discouraged by the results of their initial portfolio experiments. The problem seemed to be one of perspective and extremely high standards. We often felt teachers were harsh on both themselves and their students. This was particularly true in the older grades. Elementary teachers, especially early elementary, were generally more patient as they and their students tried new activities. It was not uncommon for us to see success and possibilities when teachers were seeing failures and problems. Such discrepancies always reminded us of the value of multiple perspectives.

SOME COMMON PROBLEMS WITH EXPERIMENTING IN THE CLASSROOM

There are a number of problems that are common with experimentation and trying new activities in the classroom. Time perhaps is the biggest problem. Experiments, even small ones, have a way of taking physical and mental energy and more time than there is to spare. Planning takes time. Talking with colleagues takes time. Doing activities takes time. Studying what happened and evaluating the experiment take time. Unfortunately, teachers are seldom able to leave other responsibilities in order to devote more time to new work.

Experiments usually require adjustment and refinement before they begin to work. Numerous teachers talked with us at length about the many versions of instructions and questions for reflections they went through before getting ones they felt were effective. Often it takes practice and repetition before students get the point and the knack of activities such as writing reflections or choosing pieces for their portfolios. Many students think portfolios are stupid until they have seen them completed, presented them to parents and strangers and had people respond to them. The strangeness of actually participating in one's own assessment can take considerable getting used to for many students, especially older ones. They may not really believe that their opinions are seriously being considered.

SHARING THE PRACTICAL EXPERIENCE OF THESE EXPERIMENTS

Knowing how to begin work with portfolios is often confusing for a school staff. One of the advantages of starting with small experiments in each teacher's classroom is that within the first months, virtually every teacher in the school will be engaged, albeit to different degrees, in serious explorations of new approaches to assessment. Many of those approaches will involve some aspect of portfolio work. So, while no one may be "doing portfolios" right off, the staff as a whole will, in all likelihood, be exploring virtually every aspect of classroom work with portfolios. It is exciting to find a dozen or twenty or forty distinct experiments in portfolio assessment going on in a school. Everyone shares what they are doing and learning. Each person's successes and failures contribute to a growing collective wisdom about assessment if they are allowed the time to talk and share, present and question, analyze and speculate.

Eventually, the small group collaborations join to larger school-wide conversations that share and discuss the results of the classroom experiments. These whole staff sessions also need to be regular although not nearly as frequent. Twice a year might suffice for these opportunities for sharing experiments and findings among the whole staff.

In these sessions, each person should make a short presentation on the developments in portfolio work in their classroom, some of what was learned from their experiments and future directions they may pursue. It is impractical to have extended conversation about specific experiments. The goal is to clarify the range of experimentation being conducted, to draw out patterns to the experiments, and to shape the direction for a school-wide portfolio practice. This planning must be updated and revised periodically to prevent the group's sense of progress and direction from becoming vague.

To end this chapter, we present one teacher's reflections on her experiences experimenting with portfolio activities in her classroom. Through her account, one can follow the evolution of her thinking and how she reshaped her experiments as she went along. Cathy Skowron is a second grade teacher at Veterans Memorial Elementary School in Provincetown, Massachusetts. In this excerpt from an interview, she discusses her reasons for starting work with portfolios. She describes the activities in her classroom that she wished to document with portfolios and her experiments over the last three years doing just that.

CATHY SKOWRON, SECOND-GRADE TEACHER

The year I came back after a year away from teaching (to go to school) was the year the school started portfolios. I had been reading over the summer some of the philosophical stuff behind it, Howard Gardner's theory of Multiple Intelligences. I had always been concerned with the kids who weren't linguistic anyway and felt that these kids are struggling and they get left behind. Here was a chance for me to say, "OK, I can experiment, I can try different kinds of things, we're all going to be working on this together. And if I want to have my classroom structured so that the kids get experiences in as many different intelligences as possible, how am I going to keep track of that?" Much of the linguistic stuff is often accompanied by worksheets, logs, etc. But if I wanted to shift focus and give weight to the non-linguistic activities that kids do, I needed a way to document this.

How do I have proof that they've done an activity? How am I going to document it for parents that the kids are actually doing work? How am I going to document it for myself that the kids are doing their curriculum? The stuff that I have to do in second grade is written up in the curriculum, and I can implement it any way I want. How can I open up the implementation so that it accommodates different styles or approaches to their learning?

That's where I got the idea for the work receipt. Here's a way for the kids to be responsible for documenting. I don't know where the idea came from. It was just one of those things that came in to my head and I tried it out and it seemed to work. The original one, when I was teaching kindergarten and first grade, didn't have that much writing on it. It was merely a drawing, in which they were asked to draw what they were working on, and there was a small written component. But that evolved as the kids developed their language and their writing through the year to include more written responses.

Later that year, in January, (my first year of teaching

second grade and doing work receipts), I switched them to using a written form in which they wrote about what they were doing in their daily activities. But they rebelled against it. They insisted that it was much harder and they didn't like it. What I found out was that I'd have to go back and say to them, "I don't understand what you did or how you did it, and I don't understand what you learned from doing this. If you are playing with the blocks for a while and you are telling me this has to do with social studies I don't see the connection." That's when I put in three questions: What did you do? How did you do it? What did you learn? They could still do the drawing component if they wanted to.

The reason I changed it was that I kept asking them those questions (see above three questions) over and over again every time they brought me a work receipt and I feel like it really told what had been going on. I found myself asking the same three questions. "Tell me more. What were you really doing? How did you do that? And what did you learn about it?" I finally wondered, why keep repeating myself? Why not just put it on the work receipt and let them address those three questions, also leave a space for the kids who wanted to do an illustration, too?

And [the class that I tried this new form on, my first year of teaching second grade] insisted it was much harder. I'm not sure why. They never could explain it. I said to them, "They are the same questions I was making you answer anyway, except now I put it in writing and before I just had to keep repeating them to you." They said "we don't know why, but we just don't like it."

Last year's class, who saw this form right from the beginning, their problem was mainly at the beginning of the year. They were just coming from first grade and they were still young academically in lots of areas so they told me that, "It's hard for us but we know we're going to get better at it." We talked about how I could make it easier for them. What do we need to do? And they said, "The more we read, the more we write and the more practice we have thinking about these questions, the easier it's going to be." I told them that they didn't have an option here, that they were going to [fill out these work receipts], and that they were right; all those things are going to help. They were just worried at first that they didn't have enough words. That's what they told me: "I don't have enough words to answer these questions." I agreed with them. The more you think about it and the more you talk about it, the easier it's going to be for you.

It was important to understand what they were writing, partly for communication. I felt that if they were doing something that they thought was valid learning, they needed some way to communicate that, whether it was to me or to their parents, verification that something was really going on there. The kids wanted this right away, too. Some of the kids from this year and the following year of teaching second grade have talked about it on their videotapes, another record-keeping device I use, about what the work receipts mean to them. They said they had proof of what they learned, and they don't remember what they did in first grade. But now they have these work receipts and the portfolios and it keeps track for them the kinds of things they've done and learned all year. So they say, "Well I can look back on this in a couple of years and I'll have proof and I know it will help me remember the kinds of things I did and what I learned."

I feel that this is important because if I want them to be motivated and involved in their work, they need to know why they're doing it, what's the outcome, who's going to see this, why is it important, why are you here, what's the reason for all this stuff. In the past three years, whenever we have an idea for a social studies topic, I ask them what they think. Is this something they want to do?

At the beginning of the year, the kids don't have the vocabulary, they don't have the language, they are not used to thinking in that way a lot, so they need some practice with it. So you start off with the work receipts, a kind of daily reflection on an activity, and they get used to thinking about what they are doing and what they might have learned about it. At the end of the week (weekly assessments) they get used to thinking about themselves in terms of the whole week about their learning and answering "why" questions about that. Sort of gradually working into it. I think around January of this year, I changed the end-of-the-week reflections to focus on "attitudes and approaches" (one of the four dimensions for assessment). So instead of saying "I was really proud of my reading this week because I got it done," I tried to get beyond that part and say, "Well what about the way you approached your reading or the way you did it made you most proud of it?" So that they would have to think [more deeply]: the kids might respond, "I really wanted to try something harder and so I looked at something that I thought was hard and found a spot by myself where I could concentrate and focus, or I sat with someone who I knew could help me read it if there were some words I didn't know." That was very difficult for them at first, but we stuck with that all winter long, up until March.

I could see it was hard and I didn't want to just do it once and say, OK we've tried that. I really thought that if they practiced...it's like practicing any other skills. . . If we have practice thinking about "attitudes and approaches"—like how or why you do your work in a certain way—then they'll learn more about themselves that way too. I think that makes a difference in their own assessment of themselves. So a lot of them came to some really important conclusions and found out some important information about themselves by doing that; they didn't always like it but they did it.

Chapter 3

COLLABORATIVE ASSESSMENT: EXAMINING AND EVALUATING STUDENT WORK

Gathering teachers together to investigate individual pieces of children's school work facilitates the identification of children's accomplishments and interests as well as their difficulties and misconceptions. Looking carefully at children's work is at the center of assessing portfolios.

The central purpose of this practice is to look carefully at the work children produce, articulating what can be seen, so that each participant's powers of clinical observation are expanded, and his sensitivity to the seriousness of the child's intent is enhanced.

ASSESSMENT AS AN INVESTIGATION

In schools, assessment is most commonly thought of as the assignment of some form of judgment by teachers on the work children produce. Certainly these judgments are a critical element of a teacher's responsibility. At key points, students need to know whether they are on the right track, whether their studying is paying off, whether they are doing very well, well enough or not well at all. At some point we all measure ourselves and are measured by others in relation to standards that exist outside ourselves. We may not agree with or even understand those standards but we must come to terms with them.

Assessment also can be conceptualized quite differently without ignoring or denying the importance of making judgments. It can be thought of as an investigation into how children learn, what they learn, and how the things they make express their understanding of the world. This kind of investigation neither starts nor ends with the assignment of judgments. It starts with careful reading of the things children make and questions about the work and the child. It ends with consideration of ways to extend and encourage children's learning.

The practice of collaborative assessment is built on the notion that assessment is, first and foremost, an investigation. This practice requires structured conversations by groups of educators about children's work. The purpose is to learn about individual children, groups of children, their interests and "what they are working on." Collaborative assessments start with consideration of a specific child's work but often lead to discussions of pedagogy and curriculum, the nature of work in a particular discipline, issues of development, ways of learning, and how children develop standards for their work.

CREATING ENERGY OR CONVERTING ENERGY?

In an after-school meeting at the Rindge School of Technical Arts (R.S.T.A.) in Cambridge, Massachusetts, the 11 staff and administrators had spent nearly half an hour reading over a set of papers from six students in the automotive class. Their teacher, Jimmy Delena, had asked these students to write a description of all of the steps they had gone through in their class project to design and build an electric vehicle. They all had difficulty with the assignment and the staff was deeply engaged in trying to understand why the task had proven so troublesome.

One teacher argued that the work was proof that vocational teachers couldn't even begin to address the enormous needs students had as writers. If, he argued, the vocational teachers were to really deal with all of the thinking and writing problems students had, they would never get to the vocational curriculum. Despair was settling over the room when another teacher, Phil, discovered yet another problem.

In reading through the student papers a second time, he noticed that three of the six students talked about the problem of how to "create the energy" needed to run their cars. When he brought this to the attention of the group, most people were at a loss to see what the problem was with this statement. Phil reminded the group that energy is not "created, it is converted." That half of the students were pursuing the design of alternative energy vehicles with a fundamental misconception about the nature of energy was, Phil argued, a serious problem.

Suddenly, a whole new set of questions was being raised. Why don't these high school kids already know this science? Didn't they ever learn about energy? If the project had to be stopped to teach basic principles of science, how would the electric car project ever get finished? This was strikingly like the problem with writing. How can you teach your subject adequately if you have to teach writing and science at the same time? If we try to teach about energy conversion, won't we need a science teacher there in the classroom?

The teachers at R.S.T.A. were engaged in an unusual activity, one that is rarely practiced in America's public schools. In an effort to use precious staff meeting time to explore critical questions of teaching and learning, Adria Steinberg, the academic coordinator, built this meeting around the activity of group "readings" of student work. She didn't know in advance what issues would emerge but she trusted that whatever emerged from the careful reading of student work would lead to consideration of serious teaching and learning issues the staff were facing in their classrooms. These issues would not emerge in the abstract. They would be direct, specific and undeniable. She wasn't disappointed.

MAKING ASSESSMENT COLLABORATIVE

The R.S.T.A. teachers could have waited until the end of the term to give a test that might or might not have shown that students had basic misconceptions about energy. But the end of the term is certainly too late. Besides, the students were offering important information about how they understood the issue of energy conversion without even being asked. In a sense, they were naming the key concepts in the study. But their teacher might well have missed this revelation because he was focused on the trouble his students were having with his assignment. It was only through the diverse perspectives and varied expertise of a dozen professional colleagues that this discovery was made. And how was Jimmy to respond in the classroom the next day? Instead of being overwhelmed by the complex decisions this revelation made him face, Jimmy had his colleagues to help sort through his options.

Collaboration as an Antidote to Isolation

The whole enterprise of assessing children's work has either been treated as the private domain of the classroom teacher or as an activity so complex and important that teachers have been completely removed from the design and assessment of these tests. It became clear to us through informal surveys that hardly any school staff allocates meeting time on a regular basis for discussion of specific pieces of student work.

Some teachers are quite content with their approaches to assessment and some of those approaches are quite innovative. Many other teachers are frustrated with the arbitrariness of their own practices and the utter lack of discussion of this most delicate aspect of teaching. For many teachers, the task, combined with isolation, is a terrible burden. Practitioners in virtually all other professions have ongoing methods of development and enrichment that rely on consideration of specific cases. The foremost purpose of making this practice collaborative is to break down this isolation by bringing teachers together on a regular basis to look at and talk together about children's work.

MARY BECK, SECOND-GRADE TEACHER
● ●

Last year it hit me over and over again how much I enjoyed doing those types of activities with other people. There were times that I would walk into these meetings, in which we would look at student portfolios from each other's classrooms, and say "I have nothing to say." Then someone would say something and something would "click" in me, an idea that I don't know I would have thought of on my own.

Collaboration Draws on Diverse Perspectives and Expertise

Children's work is complex. The more perspectives and expertise brought to consideration of a child's painting, writing, model or performance, the greater the likelihood that the complexity of the work will be recognized, acknowledged to the child and kept in mind in the planning of subsequent classroom activities. Some forms of teacher expertise are predictable. In an elementary school staff, for example, there will be people who have extensive experience with children of different ages. There also will be teachers with special knowledge of particular subject areas. No teacher is equally experienced and knowledgeable in all disciplines. When the teachers at R.S.T.A. discussed what students had written about designing electric cars, one teacher's particular interest in science drew everyone else's attention to an aspect of the work that previously eluded them.

Often the work of a particular student will tap one reader's experience and expertise in unusual and unexpected ways. In a recent group assessment session at the Atrium School, an elementary school in Watertown, Massachusetts, several teachers were captivated by a phrase in a student essay that they found particularly "poetic." After several references to the unique word choice this student had made, another teacher suggested an alternative interpretation. Almost apologetically, she suggested that the student's word choice and phrasing reminded her of some of the awkward phrasings she used when she was learning English as her second language. She wondered if this student could be an ESL student and, if so, perhaps she needed help understanding this peculiarity of English phrasing. Indeed, the child was not a native English speaker and her parents spoke Portuguese at home. While her teacher was well aware of her linguistic history, he was helped by his colleague to see this particular manifestation of his student's difficulties with English.

The participation of teachers across multiple grade levels has proven over and over to be a tremendously important element of collaborative assessment practices. It turns out that few teachers ever have occasion to look carefully at work from children older or younger than those they teach. Such limited exposure for teachers' developmental perspective is terrible. Consider the teaching of writing. If a teacher only sees the work of second graders, it is virtually impossible to place that work in a developmental framework and make the many judgments that must be made about the appropriateness of a child's progress. Collaborative assessment provides a completely natural way for teachers to investigate developmental aspects of work in any discipline.

Collaboration with Domain Experts and Educators from Outside the School

Participation in collaborative assessment practices does not need to be limited to those already in a school. When these conversations are scheduled well in advance, it is easy to invite people from outside the school who have experience and expertise that is different from those inside the school. These guests can add to the investigations of student work in a variety of ways.

In schools with diverse student populations, often there are few staff members who share culture and background with all students. A group of teachers born in this country can only speculate on what an immigrant Cambodian girl feels is appropriate to share in her writing with her teachers. Someone from her community, however, might be able to offer extraordinary insights into that child's effort and intent.

In Pittsburgh, when we were doing our initial work with collaborative assessment practices, we brought playwrights and stage directors to the sessions in which we were looking at students' original plays. In Gloucester, we brought a poet to a session when we were discussing children's poetry. These guests brought expertise but were not treated with deference. They joined the conversation. Their perspectives were welcome but not taken as sacred. Everyone brought insight. There is no single right answer in a complex investigation of children's work. In fact, absolute answers are antithetical to the work. The goal is to delve deeply and raise questions.

MAKING COLLABORATIVE ASSESSMENT A PRACTICE

Like the other practices described in this book, this is not a one-shot, in-service kind of activity. This is a fundamental professional activity characterized by deep respect for children and for the multiple perspectives and experiences of the staff. In many ways, this practice is much like the practicing of scales for a pianist. It is a basic exercise that a professional returns to time and again throughout her career. Over time, the meaning and value of the practice change and deepen while the activity remains essentially the same.

In our experience, a monthly session in which there is time to discuss two or three pieces of work is ideal. Obviously, in many schools it is hard to arrange sessions for much longer than forty minutes. Since it takes that much time to get organized and discuss a single piece of work, it is good if short sessions could be held more frequently than once a month. The sessions have to be long enough and frequent enough to allow the rigorous and in-depth examination of the presented work.

In reconsidering assessment practices, we are reconsidering many aspects of teachers' work and development. Imagine a new teacher starting work in a school where children's work is assessed collaboratively on a monthly basis, eight or nine times a year, year after year. From the beginning of her career, she has the benefit of listening to her more experienced colleagues discuss specific examples of work. She sees work from other classrooms often and notices not only what the child has done but the teacher's assignment as well. She sees work from students both younger and older than her students so she is regularly reminded of where her students are coming from and where they are going in the development of their skills, understandings and world view. Occasionally she presents work from a student in her class. These sessions make her nervous and she is glad to find out that everyone feels nervous when they present work from their classroom. After those sessions, though, she is glad that so many colleagues found it interesting to look at and discuss her student's drawings. They helped her think about this child and to reconsider her responses to another child as well.

In Gloucester, Massachusetts, ten teachers from the Fuller Elementary School participated in an experiment with collaborative assessment conferences. We met for eighteen hours over five sessions. There was time for a conference on work from every teacher's classroom. The intent was to explore what was difficult and what was rewarding about repeating this practice as a group. In addition, we wanted to see what kinds of issues would emerge in our conversations and how teachers' thinking about children as writers and children's writing might be affected. Two teachers presented some of their findings to a session at the New England Regional Assessment Network.

ELLEN SIBLEY, FIRST-GRADE

• •

It was an interesting process we went through in looking at children's writing. In the last sessions, we really came to a sense of the child's voice in the writing and ways of looking at that voice and discussing that voice. So we graduated from punctuation and spelling and visual kinds of things, to honing in on the child's voice, which was wonderful to be a part of.

JULIE CARTER, COMBINED FIRST-AND SECOND-GRADE TEACHER

• •

When you have an impression, pushing yourself beyond that to describe the information that you get from the page is really hard work. For example, what is it that gives you that impression? It affects your teaching and the way you talk to children. It affected mine. I started asking, "Tell me what you did." I asked other kids what they saw in a particular child's writing. I was more tuned into their thinking after going through the process of collaborative assessment. The whole process became so internalized that it is now a natural part of the way I look at children's work.

Again, as with so much else we are discussing in this book, traditional school schedules don't easily accommodate such conferences and schedules cannot be changed easily. But our experience suggests that it won't work to wait for the schedule to change before you try this practice. At first, these kinds of collaborative assessment sessions may have to be fit into currently allocated, already overcrowded staff meetings. Administrators may have to carve out new corners of time for these practices slowly. Over time, however, teachers and administrators must agree to rebuild the schedule to provide at least minimal time for conducting these practices.

WHY A STRUCTURE FOR THIS PRACTICE

When we began conducting group assessment sessions with our colleagues in the Pittsburgh Public Schools in 1987, we noticed a number of patterns and dynamics. In these sessions, language arts teachers brought samples of the dialogues and scenes students had written during their playwriting units. The conversations often started with the teacher who brought the work making comments about his opinion of the work and information about the student. Often teachers prefaced their comments with judgments or opinions about the quality of the work. Over and over, comments began with "I really liked..." or "I don't like when kids do this kind of writing." Sometimes the participants pointed to specific aspects of the text, other times they didn't.

We felt that the conversations weren't going as far as—or in the direction—we wanted them to go. We wanted these sessions to examine student writing and reveal as much as possible about the child, the writing process, the writer's intention and accomplishments. What mattered was what we could learn about the writer and the teaching and learning of writing. We decided to experiment with several rules for these sessions. First, we asked that the presenting teacher make absolutely no comments about the work or the child until everyone had a chance to read and discuss the work. Second, we asked the readers to focus their comments on descriptions of what the child had put in the work. We asked everyone to withhold judgments. We wanted everyone to participate and we didn't want one person's perceptions to be considered more important than anyone else's.

Almost immediately, the character and quality of the sessions changed. The first striking difference was that pieces of work that seemed very slight and hardly worthy of extended examination were turning out to be extremely interesting and provoking many questions. These questions were not only for and about the student writers but also about how writers develop their craft and what the demands of a particular genre really are.

The presenting teachers invariably had a difficult time keeping quiet for so long. It was scary to only listen to what colleagues had to say about their student's work and not be able to respond. Midway through the discussion, of course, they did get to speak, answering questions, adding observations and raising questions as well. In the end, they found these conversations both confirming and challenging. We found these conversations far more productive and insightful. Judgment, alas, seemed to say something about the reader but little about the writing.

Over a year, we experimented with rules for these discussions and evolved a protocol called "collaborative assessment conferences" which is described in detail later in this chapter. In time, we began to use this protocol for investigating other forms of children's work at various grade levels. We have had conferences around children's paintings, maps, dioramas, science projects, journals, videos of dances and other performances, math problem solving, and more. While we continue to refine the protocol, many elements remain the same—a withholding of judgments, a focus on description of the work, generating questions, speculation [based on evidence in the work] on what the child is working, and consideration of responses to the child that will encourage him to continue his efforts.

The structure of this practice ensures certain qualities to these discussions and guarantees each participant a voice. No one is given greater authority than others to observe, question or interpret the work. The presenting teacher is a learner first and explainer second. There is usually no need for the presenting teacher to ever feel like a defender of the work since there is so little value given to judgments.

ELLEN SIBLEY, FIRST GRADE TEACHER
••

Using the protocol gave teachers a way of looking at student writing where the benefit was not necessarily learning to evaluate the child but rather learning the language of assessing and what we could all gain from collaboration with each other. It's not unlike going to a city you are unfamiliar with for the first time. You have to think about what you are going to do or what it looks like when you get there. But, when we, as teachers, used the protocol it allowed us to develop a mental road map for a way of looking at children's writing so that each time we revisited a child's writing, we became enriched. We had a way of looking at it that continued to make sense. It always brought us back on track.

COLLABORATIVE ASSESSMENT CONFERENCES

Collaborative assessment conferences (CACs) are only one structure for the collaborative discussion of children's work. We describe it in some detail here as a model. We encourage experimentation with it, but whether used or not, it is presented to raise certain points and questions. Adaptations are appropriate and other models should be investigated and tried out as well.

How Collaborative Assessment Conferences Work

A CAC is a formal reading of a single piece of student work or a portfolio by a small number of teachers. Most conferences take approximately forty-five minutes but this can vary. In general, it is good to have at least five participants but good conversations can include up to ten. More can be accommodated, but it is a better idea to break a larger group into two or more smaller groups. If you were to walk in on a collaborative assessment conference-in-progress, you would see a group of teachers and administrators sitting around a large table covered with children's writings or paintings, models, maps or science notebooks, The several-hour discussion is intense but everyone takes turns, with much attention to the details of the work being examined.

Participants share doubts and confusion, questions and insights as they examine the work. These are not scoring sessions and speed is not a premium. There will probably be no final judgment in a form that could be noted and reported. There may be some consensus, but there will probably be a number of unanswered questions. This is an opportunity for teachers to explore and examine children's work. When practiced regularly, as in Gloucester, we found that this practice can, sometimes quite significantly, change the way teachers think about children and their work, assessment, and learning.

Roles in Collaborative Assessment Conferences

Each participant has one of three particular roles: the **presenting teacher, the facilitator**, or **a reader**. The assignment of each participant to a particular role should be rotated so that as many teachers as possible get to present work from their classrooms and, over time, everyone accepts the responsibility of being facilitator.

The responsibilities for each role are as follows:

The **presenting teacher** brings and presents the work of one student from her classroom. The teacher may bring the work from one project or a series of projects depending on the time available for the conference. These may include any relevant supporting materials including reflections, logs, photos, videos, various drafts and any other documentation of the process the student went through in the course of the project.

The **readers** read and discuss the student work with the perspective of informed colleagues.

The **facilitator** convenes the session, keeps track of time, asks for clarification when necessary, and for "evidence in the work" of points made by participants. The facilitator also suggests when the conversation is ready to move into its next phase.

Structure of Collaborative Assessment Conferences

Collaborative assessment conferences follow a very structured format. At each assessment conference, one teacher presents the work of a single student, distributing copies of the
work to everyone attending. The session begins with a careful,
silent reading of the work and during that time the presenting
teacher makes no comments about the child or the work itself.
In addition to the presenting teacher, the conference consists of
four other readers, one of whom is assigned the role of facilitator. Other faculty members who are attending the conference sit
outside the circle of the five participants and do not join in the
conversation until the conference is officially ended. This "fish-
bowl" structure can be used to demonstrate a CAC to an entire
school faculty.

After everyone has read the student work silently, the
three readers begin to discuss what they have read, and again
during this conversation the presenting teacher remains silent.
The readers begin by describing different aspects of the work
that attract their attention. As this descriptive phase continues,
details and nuances are explored. Anything the student has created is worth noting, even random or inconsequential elements,
such as marks, scribbles, and cross-outs.

Eventually, the facilitator asks the readers to begin to
articulate the questions the work raises for them. Deciding when
the description phase is finished and questions should begin is
not always straightforward. In most cases, the facilitator should
push the readers for more description. Often, descriptions slow
down, then, when given time, begin to build again.

In the next phase, the readers ask questions. Their questions can be about the assignment, the course of study, the
child's ideas and understandings, the child's process in making
this piece of work, or issues of interpretation and meaning. They
can be questions that would ultimately be addressed to the
child, the teacher, or those that would simply redirect attention
back to the work. We find repeatedly that the act of description

raises questions key to approaching children's work with curiosity and openness. In this way, clinical assessment becomes an investigative more than a judgmental activity.

At this stage in our collaborative assessment practices, the "presenting" teacher is asked to address a series of questions. Do you have any additional observations about the child's work to add to what your colleagues have already noted? For which assignment did the child do this work? Describe the child at work on this piece or any relevant information about the child's attitude about the piece. What do you see the child focusing on in this piece? Is there anything else you have to add to this conversation?

The final phase of the protocol asks the presenting teacher and the readers to consider possible responses and teaching moves based on this conversation. The goal of this part of the discussion is to help the teacher weigh possibilities and consider her purposes in responding. Again, we consider this a clinical protocol since it is focused so specifically on how careful investigation of a child's work can provide a basis for making pedagogical decisions.

THE FIVE STEPS IN A COLLABORATIVE ASSESSMENT CONFERENCE

1. **Read or observe the work** (pictures, videos, charts, models, writing, etc.). This is done silently; discourage casual comments. Give each person enough time to consider seriously what is in front of them.

2. **The readers speak.** Taking turns for each person to comment, the readers address the following questions.

   - What do you see in this work? Describe in the simplest and most straightforward language some aspect of what is on the page. In other words, describe what the student has created.
   - What questions about this work and the creator does your reading of this work raise for you?

- What do you think this child was working on most ardently in this piece? Identify what in the work itself leads you to this conclusion.

3. **The presenting teacher speaks.** Having listened silently up to this point, the presenting teacher comments on the following:

   - Do you have any additional observations about the work?
   - Please address some of the questions raised by the readers to which you have full or partial answers.
   - Please describe the child at work on this piece.
   - Is there anything else you want to add at this time?

4. **Strategies for response in the classroom are discussed.** The presenting teacher is asked if the conference so far has provoked any thoughts about supporting and challenging this student as she goes on with her work. The readers are asked if they have thoughts about ways in which this teacher might encourage and extend this child's engagement with her work. This discussion of next steps in working with this child and perhaps the rest of the class might consider future assignments, types of responses to the child, and techniques for gathering more information to guide pedagogical moves.

5. **The facilitator draws the session to a close.** When the conversation has come to a natural conclusion or shortly before time has run out, the facilitator draws the conference to a close, and thanks all of the participants. The facilitator then calls for a time for reflection, asking if anyone has a comments on the session. This is no longer time for discussing the work itself. It is time for consideration of the protocol and the experience of participating in the conference.

Part Three

PORTFOLIO PRACTICES ACROSS CLASSROOMS

In Part Three, we discuss three more portfolio practices. Establishing a common language and a theoretical base for implementing portfolio assessment is a critical piece of the portfolio process. Equally important is the creation of ways of actually assessing the portfolios that children create. While teachers create ways of reviewing and reporting on portfolios within their classrooms, there is also an opportunity to examine samples of portfolios from across the school. These samples will provide a striking picture of what children are doing in school—what they have to show for their time in the building and what that work shows about what they have learned.

Finally, there must be a reaching beyond the school yard. Attention must be paid from the earliest phases of implementation to how various members of the school community are informed and involved in portfolio work. Further, teachers will need to reach beyond the school walls to learn from colleagues and other models.

To these ends, we examine the following practices:

Chapter 4, **Sharing Language and Ideas**, examines the importance of regular discussions among staff and community members about the theoretical base for working with portfolios and negotiation of 'working definitions' of common terms associated with alternative assessments.

Chapter 5, **Bi-focal Assessment**, discusses the use of portfolios to assess individual children and school programs.

Chapter 6, **Protecting and Sustaining Innovation**, explores ways to inform and build support among parents and other members of the school community for innovations in assessment practice.

Chapter 4

SHARING LANGUAGE AND IDEAS

Underlying the use of portfolios for assessment are many ideas and theories about children, learning, and teaching. The explicit exploration of these ideas is an effective way of ensuring that teachers develop a deep and critical sense of the purposes and values of portfolio assessment. Further, the language of assessment is full of terms that have multiple and sometimes contradictory meanings. Moving forward with portfolios demands that the staff agree on working definitions for these terms. Again, this process must be explicit, negotiated and documented.

WORKING DEFINITIONS

While the last few years have seen a tremendous increase in teachers' conversations about portfolio assessment, there are often as many different ideas about what a "portfolio" is as there are participants in the conversation. To an art teacher, the portfolio is often a collection of "best pieces" that could be used for admission to a school of the arts, application for a design job, or to land a gallery showing. To a writing teacher, a portfolio might be a record of the development of individual pieces as well as, in sum, a portrait of an emerging writer. To a principal, portfolios may be a collection of data that can be examined to get a picture of how students as a whole are doing in a particular subject. All of these ideas about "portfolios" are reasonable and appropriate in different contexts. Each of these three educators may publicly support the use of portfolios. Yet a conversation among them about a specific issue, such as like what the contents of a portfolio should be, is likely to become bogged down and quite confusing.

There are often very different understandings of what is meant by terms like "standards" or "authentic assessments." Nearly every term commonly used in discussions of assessment seems to have multiple meanings. On a regular basis we found that when staff discussions became contentious or just plain hard to follow, progress was poor because people were talking different languages, or, more precisely, the same language but with very different meanings.

A recent publication about portfolios gave definitions for over twenty-five terms used frequently in conversations about portfolios and other forms of assessment. Virtually every term on this list was a source of confusion to us at some time. Countless hours had gone into debating these meanings in our meetings and many of these debates became quite hot. We admired the effort that had gone into this glossary but doubted we would use such a list in our work with school staffs for two major reasons. First, short definitions of these terms seemed to flatten the vitality and complexity of their meanings and we were concerned that the glossary would close discussion rather than encouraging it. Second, agreeing on "working definitions" leads everyone involved to a shared understanding of the group's conversation. Assigning meaning to language is a fundamental activity of a vital community. When it is undertaken successfully, it confirms the community's authority and control over its actions and its understandings.

This is a significant challenge for any staff implementing portfolio assessment. In short, it isn't simply that it is better for a staff to define its terms rather than be forced to accept someone else's definitions; the latter is rarely a successful enterprise. Meanings are too subjective and complex to be mandated with ease. For a group to share definitions of common words and terms, there is no substitute for the often time-consuming effort of talking through the meanings of words and coming to agreements.

This effort, however arduous it may be, can have significant payback. Colleagues are forced to grapple with differences in their thinking and perspectives. Coming to a working definition is far less a process of determining that one person is right and another is wrong than negotiating and building consensus. This process draws teachers closer to the thinking of their colleagues. In turn, participants become more aware of their own ideas and the relationship of those ideas to the practice.

For some people these conversations are difficult. They think that this activity isn't productive and time for staff to be together is too precious to argue definitions. Isn't this, these people argue, simply re-inventing the wheel? The criticism is implicit. The wheel has been around for a long time. It works. We don't have time to waste. Let's get on with our work.

Experience tells us that this practice is much more than re-inventing the wheel. It is making a commitment to understanding what a wheel is, its infinite varieties and uses in different situations and to making everyone involved in rolling capable of designing the wheel even if they didn't do it in the first place.

In the following story, an elementary school's staff had to find out what other people meant when they talked about alternative assessments, come up with their own working definitions and quickly make a plan of action. The meeting had a clear agenda and was well prepared for. It led directly to a new initiative for the public presentation and review of the portfolios of all graduating sixth-graders.

A Short Story of Clarifying Language and Ideas

Suddenly, near the end of two years of work with portfolios in their elementary school, all of the teachers in one of our collaborating schools received a memo from the superintendent explaining that he had decided the district should move toward assessment by exhibition. Confusion and considerable anxiety ensued. What would happen to all of their work with portfolios? What are exhibitions, anyway? Are portfolios and exhibitions mutually exclusive?

The staff asked us to come to a meeting and explain what exhibitions are. We agreed to do this and then realized that we didn't really understand exhibitions. We weren't really sure what was similar and different about portfolios, exhibitions and performance tasks. So we called everyone we knew who had worked with these approaches to assessment, gathered examples and definitions and started to explore the distinctive qualities of each.

With articles, charts and video tapes, we headed out to a two-hour meeting with the staff. Their concern was understanding all they could about exhibitions so that they could define their own approach to using them for assessment. They wanted to be proactive, not wait for a district definition to be handed down. Together, we examined these examples and made a giant chart of the qualities of, advantages to, and differences between each of these approaches to assessment. We talked at length about what teachers already do that could be interpreted as exhibitions and performance assessments. By the end of the meeting, we had some pretty clear ideas about the relationship between portfolios and exhibitions and the beginnings of a plan for natural and comfortable ways the elementary school could begin to incorporate elements of assessment by exhibition without compromising their investment in portfolios. The staff was ready to move forward and significantly less anxious than when they began.

THE IDEAS BEHIND ANY APPROACH TO ASSESSMENT

Conversations about assessment seem to have a way of bringing to the surface teachers' different assumptions about critical issues such as children's roles in their learning, teachers' roles in assessment, the relationship of assessment and learning, and how children learn. These are fundamental issues in schooling and it is no surprise that an entire staff is unlikely to share perspectives on them. Like the meaning of assessment terminology, it is likely that, without explicit discussion of disagreements and differences in perspective, the staff's ability to talk openly and productively will be significantly compromised. These ideas form the intellectual foundations for reconsidering and redesigning approaches to assessment. Educational practices built on weak or unarticulated ideas and theories are bound to falter, if not fail.

It is not the purpose of this practice to force agreements where they don't exist. Coercing teachers to think or do things in their classrooms in a particular way produces resistance and resentment. Talking about the language of assessment and the ideas behind assessments is meant, however, to call attention to differences and to create understanding of them. If this understanding leads to greater unity of thought, great. If it doesn't, fine. Individuals and the group still will be much stronger for having grappled with diverse opinions and perspectives.

Some of these conversations can be planned, especially discussions of theories and ideas. Sometimes, however, serious issues of pedagogy and assessment emerge spontaneously and should be pursued; but, they need time and a little preparation.

A Short Story of Using Research to Clarify Ideas and Questions

We were working with an elementary school. During collaborative assessment of children's writing, teachers expressed confusion and various opinions on how children learn to spell and a teacher's role in this process. Very different positions on this issue were represented in the room. (This wasn't, strictly speaking, an assessment question but assessment questions often raise issues of curriculum and instruction.)

People felt challenged and uncomfortable. How to teach spelling is a major question in elementary education. Various positions on this question reflect deeply held ideas about the development of literacy, the relationship of sound and written language, the effect of a "right and wrong" environment in the classroom, the teacher as corrector vs. teacher as reader/responder, child development, and creativity. The issue is difficult to confront directly.

We decided to read an essay that addresses this issue by Eleanor Duckworth, "The Language and Thought of Piaget, and Some Comments on Learning to Spell." It looks specifically at invented spelling. When we returned to the topic, everyone had a common reference point to ground the discussion (1987, 15-30). Duckworth's opinions could be argued more easily than those of the people in the room. The essay crystallized ideas and questions. Using the essay to further frame our questions and confusion, we were able to approach this complex issue more deeply.

We are often called on to bring research and theoretical positions to our meetings with school staffs. Many times we have discussed Howard Gardner's theory of multiple intelligences that is identified with Project Zero research and is useful in thinking through issues of diversity in approaches to learning and knowing. It is useful to draw on resources like articles, book chapters or guest speakers to help stimulate and inform discussions of theory and educational ideas. Theories of children's development directly impact approaches to work with portfolios.

We don't recommend burying teachers in articles to read. If we don't think children do well when swamped with work, why do we think teachers will? Carefully chosen pieces offered at times when particular issues are being discussed by the staff can be helpful to some people. Again, speakers and readings are not to be offered as absolute answers. They are meant as reference points and stimulants to professional conversations.

In short, the practice should engage teachers and administrators in regular and explicit discussions of the language and key ideas of portfolio assessment. Of course, these are interconnected; discussion of language implies discussion of ideas and vice versa. These discussions may be in large or small groups and will be both planned and spontaneous. In many schools, this kind of conversation may be highly unusual, while in others it may be quite familiar. Experience has shown that real progress in portfolio work is dependent on the willingness of the staff to engage collectively with the ideas behind portfolios as much as techniques for collecting or assessing them.

MAKING AND TAKING TIME

Where does the time for this kind of conversation come from in already overloaded schedules? Time must be made or taken. Taking time to talk about language and ideas can become a vital element of professional practice in a school. Before administrators and staff will make the time, active discussion and debate of ideas underlying classroom practice must be valued as a critical activity for teachers .

There are many forums in which such conversations can take place. In some schools, there are obvious settings such as assessment committees. In other schools, the time teachers come together for conversation is often so limited and the agenda so full that it is almost impossible to talk about theories and practice, language and meanings. In some schools, these conversations are part of the life-blood of the professional community. In other schools, these conversations threaten to expose deep differences in educational beliefs and values.

Many of these discussions will happen spontaneously, but they must not be prematurely dismissed. Finding the best times for this practice demands sensitivity on the part of those in charge of running meetings. Principals, team leaders, department chairpersons and other group leaders must become aware of the points at which language needs to be defined and ideas explored. Identifying these moments is one of the keys to this practice. Stepping into the conversation and asking whether there is real agreement on meanings, for example, and then guiding the surfacing of various meanings takes leadership and a commitment to ensure that everyone is a full participant in the conversation.

This practice requires leadership that is concerned with the intellectual life of the staff. This leadership also must be aware of the delicate balancing act that must be performed between taking care of business (from problems with buses to the ordering of books and on and on), dealing with issues of practice (are our programs working as well as we want?) and exploring ideas that are the foundation of practice. This takes sensitivity and commitment. It is easy to let go of or never have time for the exploration of ideas. It is the most dispensable of often competing concerns. Our time in schools revealed that as hard as it can be to make time for these conversations and as awkward as they may be to have at times, it is essential that, over time, teachers, individually, and as a group, develop a deep understanding of the ideas at the root of portfolio assessment. If portfolio assessment is to survive the ever-shifting trends of educational fashion, work with portfolios must have deep roots in a staff's ideas and beliefs.

"But that wasn't putting myself on the line. In fact, I didn't know what it meant to put myself on the line until I started having students keep a portfolio. The first time we used them I was terrified! Suddenly my judgments were really out there. With a portfolio, if I said a student did great work or lousy work, everyone and anyone could open the portfolio, look at the work and really question my judgment. I suddenly had to be able to explain why I thought the work was great or lousy, ground-breaking or lackluster. I had to have examples against which I held the work. No one could argue with my grade book but they could argue with my judgments.

"And not only that, but my whole classroom was on display in those portfolios. When another teacher or administrator looked at the portfolios, I knew that they were looking at my assignments and my feedback as much as they were looking a particular child's work! If a student wrote a boring paper, was it the student's fault or was it a crummy assignment? I've never felt more vulnerable. Part of me wanted to run and hide behind my grade book. Believe me, I was tempted. But I knew if I wanted my students to feel that their work was on the line then I had to let my work be on the line, too!"

ASSESSING PORTFOLIOS

At a recent meeting of the sixty teachers involved in the New England Regional Assessment Network, one participant, a sixth-grade language arts teacher, grew restless at the end of the day. "We say we are talking about portfolio assessment. But all I've heard all day... in fact, all I've heard at any of our meetings is talk about portfolios—what goes in them, how to get kids involved, how to document work that disappears. When are we going to talk about assessment? I mean, once you've got these portfolios, how does anyone actually assess them?"

Generally, when teachers discuss this question, they talk about assessing individual student performance or progress. But the same question can be asked about the assessment of portfolios from very different perspectives. What can be learned about a group of students, the curriculum or instruction from reading a sample of portfolios from a single classroom? What can be learned from reading a sample of portfolios from a single grade in a school, or across several grades in a school or across several schools in a district? In each case, quite different questions can be raised and they quickly cease to be about individual children. Arguably, the long-term value of portfolios depends on their use beyond the assessment of individual children within a classroom.

This is an extremely complicated matter. Many teachers and teacher groups raise serious questions about the use of portfolios to evaluate teachers. They want to know how a single child's work, or even a number of childrens' work, can be adequate evidence of a teacher's performance, the strengths and weaknesses in the whole complex job. Others question the validity of assessing a curriculum or a program (such as a new approach to teaching algebra) on the basis of student work in a sampling of portfolios. Certainly these concerns are serious. Certainly they should be argued long and hard. But just as certainly, portfolios, when examined in samples from a classroom or a school, reveal as much about a learning environment as they do about individual children.

If portfolios are to be useful in the improvement of educational practice for groups of children, they must be examined with that goal in mind. In other words, teachers have to read portfolios looking specifically at the assignments given, the balance of learning modes addressed, the nature and effectiveness of their feedback, and various other issues of curriculum and instruction. Throughout our research project, we saw time and again how individual teachers found ways to learn important lessons about their curriculum and the way they organize their classrooms in the process of reading and assessing their students' portfolios.

The rigorous demands of grading and reporting to parents keeps most teachers focused on individual children. They start by sitting down to read through a stack of portfolios in order to report on student progress or performance and, by the time they finish they see many other aspects of the classroom life. For many of these teachers, these insights lead to shifts and adjustments in their teaching.

In the schools we studied, there was little or no tradition of collaborative assessment of any style, except among team teachers. In most schools, the expectation is that principals, district personnel or even the state will handle the responsibility for using assessments (usually standardized tests) to hold the school accountable for meeting student performance standards. While few teachers like this model, there are few schools that hold themselves accountable through any kind of systematic assessment. The practice of bi-focal assessment is a step in the direction of using portfolios to full advantage, focusing on individual students at some times and on groups of students, curriculum, instruction and school programs at other times.

Imagine a middle school that has recently implemented a new pre-algebra program. There is serious concern over the appropriateness and effectiveness of this new approach. On one hand, the staff could simply look at the eighth-grade students' scores on the district-wide algebra placement exam and if most students are scoring well, the program could be considered a success. But how could any real analysis of what works and what doesn't work in the program be conducted from these test scores? On the other hand, if two or three teachers conduct a careful reading of a dozen randomly selected portfolios and then discuss a what they saw—looking for patterns, citing questions and concerns—they might well discover significant ways to improve the program. They might even come to specific and valuable insights about aspects of algebra that seem especially difficult for these students. In other words, they might come to understand the domain better while they seek to improve instruction.

What makes portfolios assessment complicated is exactly what makes them so valuable as a basis for assessing both individual children and school programs. As collections of student work, portfolios reveal as much about the school environment as they do about the child. When a child applies herself to a task in school, the product is a reflection of both the child and the task. The teacher makes the assignment. The child interprets it. The materials available for undertaking the task are there by virtue of decisions made by principals, district coordinators, parent advisory councils, financial officers, superintendents and school committees. The specific content knowledge the child brings to the effort is often, not always, the result of the principal's curriculum. The child's ideas about how to pursue a task and investigate the unknown are significantly, though not entirely, formed by the structure of all previous activities in the classroom. All of these things are reflected in the child's work. They are not always easy to decipher or interpret but they are there.

Certainly, the same work contains reflections of aspects of the child's world outside of school. It is important to acknowledge and identify these elements. They are part of the myriad factors that contribute to a child's success or failure in school. For our purposes, we will focus on the elements of the environment that teachers have some control over—curriculum, pedagogy and school programs.

MULTIPLE LENSES

Think of this process as one that requires different lenses for each aspect of what the portfolio reveals. Like looking through any new set of lenses, looking at portfolios with special focus on a particular aspect of the child or the classroom takes some getting used to. Looking at portfolios with no specific lens leaves the whole document somewhat blurry.

There are many lenses to use when reading portfolios. There can be focus on the growth or accomplishments or interests or thinking of individual children, for example. Stepping back and looking at a number of portfolios, focus can be on groups of children and issues of development, skills or understandings. Other points of focus can be on aspects of individual classrooms or aspects of a school's programs.

We include an illustration below to identify the variety of lenses through which portfolios might be assessed. Each of these lenses could reveal valuable information. Often, though, the finer the lens, the more useful the findings. There is nothing

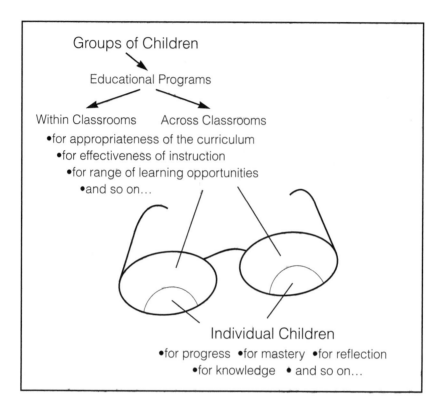

comprehensive or absolute about this chart and it is offered here both to suggest the various kinds of information portfolios can provide and to serve as a starting point for conversations about lenses for assessment. Readers are invited to add, combine, tease apart, or redefine any aspect.

Within this practice, we have tried to place many different lenses into two basic degrees of focus—individual children and groups of children. From either of these focal points, numerous finer points can be explored. In actual practice, these distinctions are rarely so neat. Focusing on an individual child often leads to insights about programs and focusing on a group of portfolios often stimulates insights about individual children. Nonetheless, we suggest these distinctions in order to highlight a critical problem. Looking at either category at the expense of the other misses the sublime possibility embedded in portfolios: They reflect both the child and the environment and therefore provide a basis for assessing both.

Every school and every teacher we have worked with confronts this complexity when assessing portfolios. For some, it is relatively easy to integrate an analysis of the evidence contained in portfolios into an existing or evolving approach to the assessment of individual children. The assessment of programs is a different matter. As discussed earlier, there are few schools in which there is ongoing, whole staff, structured assessment of student work and how to systematically and consistently improve educational practice. Portfolios can be a tremendous help in this conversation but they don't make the conversation happen. People have to decide it is right, useful, and necessary to talk about these things.

Given the many things that can be seen and assessed in portfolios, it is not surprising that many discussions of portfolios become confused and lose their bearings. The potential to explore specific issues, reach conclusions and make suggestions for improving practice becomes diffused and the opportunity for using assessment as a catalyst for change is lost. When looking at either individual children's portfolios or groups of children's portfolios, there are two preliminary steps that are useful in helping clarify and steady a reader's focus.

Declare Your Lens

What you are assessing must be named. A specific, and generally agreed upon, focus helps everyone to sort through what relevant evidence and to organize those pieces for more careful examination. It can be as difficult to focus on the whole classroom as it is to focus on the whole child. It is quite possible, though, to focus on a child's emerging literacy, as multi-faceted as that may be, or the school's whole language program. Finding the right specificity of focus takes time and practice.

There is an interesting paradox contained in this principle. On the one hand, it is important to choose a focus for a reading of portfolios. On the other hand, it is often impossible to know what can be seen in a set of portfolios before they have been carefully examined. The simple resolution: serious consideration of single or sets of portfolios will take at least two readings.

Start with Open Questions

While many assessments are guided by scoring rubrics, we suggest a slightly looser starting point for portfolio assessments of educational programs. In time, more formal frameworks may evolve in individual schools for guiding the reading and assessment of portfolios. This is wonderful when it happens as a result of an on-going process of conducting assessments, reflecting on those assessment processes and then making appropriate changes in the processes.

Initially, simple, open questions are quite adequate for starting useful conversations. These guiding questions can be established by the group just prior to the assessment session. In assessing the effectiveness of a new foreign language program, for example, effective questions will focus the reader on important forms of evidence. Is there evidence to show that students are becoming competent speakers and readers of this language? Is there evidence that students can retain knowledge of this language over long periods (two months or more)? Is there evidence that students are gaining a familiarity with the culture as well as the language? What is learned from reading these portfolios about the level of student engagement with this study of a new language?

ASSESSING INDIVIDUAL CHILDREN

There is much to explore and invent in approaching both of these categories of assessment. There may be as many approaches to the assessment of individual children through reading their portfolios as there are teachers. There seem to be certain themes that emerge in teachers' discussions of what they look for, however. Growth is, of course, a common point of assessment. Others include a child's place on a developmental continuum in various domains, a child's special interests, a child's own standards of excellence, and a child's particular approaches to learning and performing in school. We've had many conversations with teachers about what they do and what they look for when they are reading their students' portfolios.

Below are fragments from two of those conversations that indicate both the common themes mentioned above and the highly individual ways teachers think about the task of assessing children through examination of their work. The first comes from Miriam Raider-Roth, a teacher of a mixed grades 1-2 classroom at the Atrium School in Watertown, Massachusetts. Miriam was teaching with Connie Henry, and together they had been using portfolios in their classroom for several years.

The second comes from Bev Hoeltke, a second-grade teacher at the Key School in Indianapolis, Indiana.

MIRIAM RAIDER-ROTH, FIRST-GRADE TEACHER

I try to look at the portfolios with the kids in November, January, April and June. I look at them as a reflection of the child in the class. It's going to be a reflection of what the child's interaction has been with me, children, teachers and materials in the classroom. I assess his work by reporting on what I've seen over time, and I use the portfolio to help me. I use it as a source of information about this child's interaction with knowledge, with himself, with learning. I could never put a number on a portfolio because that's not what I use it for or ask the kids to use it for.

When I ask the kids to look at it I ask them to look at how they've seen themselves change or stay the same, what things they notice or what stands out in the portfolio. And I look at children's interactions with their portfolios: how do they use it, how often do they use or put things in it? There's a child in my class this year who puts everything in his portfolio; he said it's the only safe place in the classroom. That's very meaningful in terms of what that space means to him. And then there's a child who won't put anything in there at all; that is also a statement.

I don't look at a portfolio and ask, "What am I learning from the whole body," but "What am I learning from the content and the pieces that are there?" Certainly I learn something when I notice that a portfolio is fat or thin, or if everything in a portfolio has one quality about it, but most portfolios don't look like that. Certain areas stand out in terms of strength. I do look at the whole child, and the portfolio as a piece of that child.

I rate portfolios in relation to the child. I have a child who is very competent in almost every domain. In a painting project she kind of rushed right through it. I wouldn't say to her "This is a rotten piece of work; you really rushed." But it made it really clear to me that what this child needs is someone to pull the reins and say to her that even though she is good at all of this, she needs a personal challenge to slow down and go more in depth with her work.

I'm evaluating constantly. I read with a child today whose reading is markedly better than it was a month ago. I asked him if he knows how much better his reading is. He didn't have a sense of that, so I pointed out to him the areas of growth, and he was surprised. I tend to do that more with successful activities than with less successful ones. When pieces of work are milestones or statements of achievement I'll pull the child's and parents' attention to that.

BEV HOELTKE, SECOND-GRADE TEACHER
●●

I'm really interested in the development of the child and how that happens. Each child seems to follow stages, yet each child's fingerprint is unique and so a portfolio captures the uniqueness of the child, shows her strengths and her development along the way. I think that's important to know as a teacher. And I think it's important for the child and the parents to know it so that parents can provide appropriate materials and support along the way too.

I assess my portfolios for several reasons. First, I assess them to look at the child. To me, children are like puzzles and it's my responsibility as a teacher to figure out how the child learns and then to provide that instruction, especially reading and writing. So when I go through a portfolio the first time, I'm looking for clues into how the child's going to learn. I do that right at the very beginning of the year because I want to get the children into learning right away and it's my job to provide instruction. Even though the portfolios are not in a real rigid form at that point, I'm still going through them looking for clues; pictures can give me those clues, or sometimes I'll look for the child's interest, like what the child really got into and got involved with and put a lot of detail into.

I am also looking for their writing because that gives me clues as to where they are. So it gives me clues to the child's interest and then I can usually tell, like a detective, that they are sounding out words or they have no idea how to sound out words, so that will give me clues on how that child's going to learn. Then I can provide the instruction and curriculum that I feel is appropriate for them.

When I go through the portfolios I have a book that I keep that has each child's name and I might take notes on things I may need to work on. If I'm concerned specifically about one child, I'll take notes. There is no standard sheet, but there are certain categories that we base the portfolios on such as Gardner's seven intelligences, so there is a category for each one of those. Since I am personally responsible as a classroom teacher for the linguistic and mathematical part, I'm looking to make sure there is a variety of writing.

I don't use my notebook a whole lot unless I'm at wit's end on what to do; then I'll go back and review what I've written down to see if I've left anything out as far an individual child or class. I use it as a reference point to see if I've missed anything. I also read a lot of portfolio books to see if what I am doing is coinciding with what the books say. The purpose of my assessment is to basically get an understanding of the child and to help him along the continuum of learning, finding out where the child is in that moment of time.

LOOKING BEYOND INDIVIDUAL CHILDREN

When Background Becomes Foreground

In 1991, we began collecting student portfolios from elementary and middle school grades. We made the most complete and accurate copies of these portfolios with color photocopying and without reducing the sizes of the work. We made copies of videotapes and audiotapes when necessary. Our goal was to begin to build a collection of faithfully reproduced portfolios for our research and as a resource to teachers and other researchers.

Once the collection started to grow, we began systematic readings of all of the portfolios. Our initial assumption was that the portfolios would be a reflection of the children who made them and our hope was that we would be able to see important qualities of each child's learning experience and school performance. To our surprise, virtually all of the readers (none of whom actually knew the children whose portfolios were being read) emerged from the readings with far more observations and questions about the classroom and school than about the individual child. These questions revealed the importance of providing context in the presentation of portfolios to readers unfamiliar with the classroom. More importantly, when specific and explicit interest in a particular child was not a part of a portfolio reader's motive for reading, the context for the child's work no longer stayed in the background; it moved quickly and vigorously to the foreground.

This was not simply a trick of focusing. We realized in interviewing the portfolio readers about their perceptions that the portfolios were as much a reflection of the environment as of the child. When someone was reading a portfolio with a more immediate interest in issues of the quality of educational practice in a school, district or classroom than in the experience of a particular child, it was quite natural to switch focus from the child to the context—and quite revealing.

Using Multiple Portfolios to Assess Curriculum, Instruction and Learning Environments

While the assessment of individual children is no simple process, we suspect that it is undertaken, if not collaboratively, then certainly by individual teachers. The assessment of programs by school staff is another matter. We call this practice "bifocal assessment." There is no precise recipe or blueprint for this practice. It is the practice with which we have had the least experience. The schools we have worked with have only just begun to systematically explore this aspect of work with portfolios. Unfortunately, few schools have adequate staff work time devoted to careful and systematic evaluation of school programs, whether with portfolios or any other body of evidence. The evaluation of programs is generally considered the domain of administrators.

We have seen, however, the various ways in which individual teachers have been moved to reconsider significant aspects of their curriculum and their teaching as a result of reading through their students' portfolios. In the course of those readings, certain patterns emerged from the work students produced that had not been obvious earlier. Often those patterns suggested strengths and weaknesses in the learning environment.

One teacher saw clearly that certain projects her students did during the year were of consistently much higher quality than others, and she became anxious to understand why. She reviewed her approach to these different projects, talked informally with some of the students, and re-read their evaluations of these projects. Through this process it became clear to her that she had provided much more in-class work time for some projects than for others. Usually, her sense of being pressed for classroom time to cover more of the curriculum forced her to insist that students work on these other projects at home. Besides, she reasoned to herself, these students should be able to work more independently. But, in her review of the portfolios, it was abundantly clear that for most of her students, the quality of their projects was directly correlated to the amount of time devoted to working on them, talking about them and evaluating them in class. She realized that in the future she would have to make some serious choices about her expectations for quality work, the number of projects she assigned and just how much history the class would be able to cover.

Bev Hoeltke, who spoke earlier in this chapter about assessing individual children, also talks about how reading her students' portfolios influenced her thinking about her own work in her classroom.

BEV HOELTKE, SECOND GRADE

I look at all of the portfolios to get a whole picture of the class and figure out where we are going, because I look at them also for curriculum and where I should be going with the class. When I go through and read all the portfolios in a general way, I'm not looking for specific clues. During these moments, I'm looking to see the types of learning activities that my students have and have not grasped. The portfolios point me to areas that the students and I need to work on.

I do this periodically, about every nine weeks, to get a sense of the class. As far as curriculum and learning, we don't have a scope and sequence like other schools do, so it's really important for me to review the portfolios so I see if I'm hitting everything that these children are going to need. Also, since our staff has developed its own standards and criteria for assessing children's learning, I need to use those also as some kind of standard. I need to make sure that my children are actually receiving curriculum and instruction on those particular descriptors so that they are reaching the next level on the continuum.

Bev, like many other teachers, uses her portfolios to inform her teaching, but, on the whole, this is a solitary process. In a very different vein, a staff subcommittee at the elementary school in Provincetown, Massachusetts spent two weeks during the summer of 1993 reading a sample of portfolios from the fifth and sixth grades. They began this first-time enterprise by asking what they could find out about the school from reading a group of portfolios. It was not an easy task; they were very conscious that reading portfolios was similar to peering in an open window on a classroom. These teachers chose to read only portfolios from their classrooms even though every teacher in the school had left sets of portfolios with the committee.

These readings led the group into many discussions of students' experiences as they completed the last two years of elementary school. They shared concerns about the curriculum and whether students left the school prepared for junior high school. What distinguished these conversations was that these teachers kept returning to the portfolios to find evidence for their perceptions about students' work, levels of mastery and competence, ability to express themselves and solve problems. Having portfolios from a range of students allowed them to check and double check their perceptions, look for patterns, and identify the variety of experiences students have in the school.

The work of this committee was exploratory. They were inventing ways to use portfolios to inform their understanding of what the school does well and where it needs to focus attention. They had no models or guidelines. But they found the portfolios to be rich bodies of information and they emerged with a list of recommendations for the staff of ways to make group reading of portfolio samples more productive in the future.

We conclude this chapter with a brief discussion of three key ideas for initiating examination of multiple portfolios for the assessment of curriculum, instruction and school programs. Included are some guiding principles and strategies for organizing readings: 1) looking across a classroom; 2) looking across classrooms, and; 3) sampling.

Looking Across a Classroom

Some open questions may guide a teacher's reflections on her readings of all of the portfolios from her classroom. Depending on class size, it may make good sense to read only a sample from a class. Looking across a classroom, there are questions about the group of children as well as questions about curriculum and pedagogy. For instance, what activities seem to have been most enjoyable or engaging for students this term? Are there assignments on which some students did very well and others seemed unable to produce quality work? Are there patterns of success and failure across assignments or projects? What concepts did all (or most) children show evidence of grasping deeply? What can be learned about child development in any particular area or skill from my reading of these portfolios?

Looking at the curriculum and pedagogy, other questions come to mind. Having read all of these portfolios, what do I notice about my choices as a teacher—choices of assignments, decisions about how fast or slow to move the class, ways of responding to students' work, when to push and when to ease up? What pleases me? What concerns me? Are there some students I seem to be more effective with than others? And on and on.

In many respects, the ultimate value of such assessments rests on the creativity and curiosity brought to establishing these guiding questions. The ones we suggest are offered only as models. The questions you ask should be important to your work and understanding of your students.

As with other practices, the value of these "within the classroom" readings can be enhanced immeasurably by having a colleague with whom to check thoughts and perceptions. Again, this kind of collaboration benefits from structure and support. Having a time allotted for this kind of teacher self-assessment and reflection and knowing that all teachers are engaged in the same activity is strong encouragement. If there is follow-up time the value of these sessions is enhanced.

The basic rules of good listening apply. The partners or small groups may or may not have had opportunity to read portfolios from the reflecting teacher. The partners are active listeners, making notes, asking for clarification and evidence. Perhaps the most important role the listeners play is in demanding to see where in the portfolios the teacher has found evidence for thoughts or conclusions about the classroom. A mild "prove it to me" attitude can be useful. The point is always to help the reflecting teacher clarify thoughts and think toward the future, considering possible improvements or issues to work on in future months.

Looking Across Classrooms

Looking at samples of portfolios from across the classrooms in a school must be a structured activity with clear leadership. All of the problems we have discussed in this chapter will most likely present themselves. What are we trying to understand through this assessment? What is an adequate and appropriate sample of portfolios to read? Who should be a reader? And, not mentioned explicitly, but quite important, what will we do with our findings?

There are no magic formulas. The crucial step, as before, is to know what you want to learn. This may be absolutely obvious or quite difficult to determine. In either case, it must be explicit and agreed upon as important.

It may be too overwhelming to look across an entire school and come up with specific and meaningful conclusions about the effectiveness of educational programs. Looking at samples of portfolios from a specific grade or span of grades can help focus the readings. Similarly, looking at samples from a particular subject area can provide another focus. Looking at portfolios from a particular population in the school (bilingual students, for example) is another way to focus readings. The questions for these assessments cover a wide range of issues including the effectiveness of curriculum and pedagogical approaches, concerns about the allocation of time to different activities or studies, the effectiveness of school programs for all students across gender, race, class and ethnicity lines, and so on.

All members of the staff should be aware of the entire plan for any programmatic assessment of portfolios. What will be assessed and why, who will do the assessing, what procedures will be followed? Most important, what will happen with the findings of the assessment needs to be considered and publicized prior to any formal sessions. The assessment of school programs is an enormously sensitive activity. Teachers' and administrators' professional dignity and reputation are at stake. These are not witch hunts nor opportunities to place blame. These are situations in which professionals take responsibility for assessing their effectiveness and the effectiveness of their institution and make plans for improvement. All possible measures must be taken to conduct these proceedings with respect, sensitivity and rigor.

Sampling

In planning any systematic assessment of a school program, it also will be necessary to pull a sample of portfolios to read rather than attempting to read all of the portfolios. Within a classroom, of course, a teacher will read all of his students' portfolios. But to bring another teacher into the assessment of those portfolios or to read portfolios from across classrooms, a selected group of portfolios must be drawn.

Two problems stand out: How many portfolios are considered a representative sample? How should the sample be chosen? These questions have plagued (and intrigued!) quantitative researchers and psychometricians since the beginning of their respective fields.

In schools, these problems are a little easier. Practicality almost always wins the day. In general, it makes sense to read as many portfolios as readers can give adequate time and attention. In most situations, with a total of forty or more portfolios, it will be adequate to read a quarter of the total. If chosen randomly, there is a good chance of getting a representative sample.

Random choice often is a perfectly adequate method of choosing a sample. In situations where there are clear groups of students who should be represented in a sample, the whole group can be subdivided into smaller groups. At that point use random choice. Proportion representation can be easily achieved once all of the portfolios have been assigned a single group. If, for example, gender is thought to be a critical factor in the assessment, either equal or proportional numbers of girls' and boys' portfolios can be chosen. There are many choices to make.

When assessments produce unexpected findings, participants often have second thoughts about the sample. Perhaps it was too small or not representative enough. The simplest thing to do at that point is to randomly pull some more portfolios and examine them for evidence that confirms or contradicts the findings from the original sample. Again, this is only an informal way of checking the stability of findings.

Chapter 6

PROTECTING AND SUSTAINING INNOVATION

Portfolios cannot be implemented in classrooms and schools without making changes. Often, these changes are confusing and threatening to many people. To protect these new assessment practices, teachers must openly share the reasons they are experimenting with portfolios, exactly what they are asking of children, their best guesses at what the advantages and costs will be for students, and how they will assess the effectiveness of portfolios. The doors of the classroom must be opened, not closed, and all those with an interest in the children must be invited in.

"PARENTS ON BOARD?"

Consider these headlines from a small community's weekly newspaper:

*Local Teachers "Motivated, Excited" by
Conference on Test Alternatives*

*Parents Question Experimental Program
at Elementary School*

*Project Zero Draws Attention, Much Praise,
Some Criticism*

Two years of intensive work with portfolios were suddenly in jeopardy. We and the staff had thought that parents were enthusiastic about the portfolios their children were keeping. Some parents wanted to see more work coming home each week. But when they came to school and saw their child's portfolio they began to see where all that work had gone. Instead of having art work live on the refrigerator or in a box under a bed, it was being organized into folders or notebooks or boxes at school. Most important, though, the portfolios were the focus of parent conferences and conversations between children and their parents about how—and what—they were doing in school.

The school had not changed its standardized testing policy and report cards went home with grades and/or checklists as they always had. The only major change was that now when parents asked teachers to explain why their child had received a certain grade, the teacher could point to the child's work as evidence of their evaluation.

Needless to say, there was anxiety and concern about changes in the school and changes in assessment can be particularly confusing. In the end, the furor blew over but not before a special school committee meeting was held which left the entire staff feeling defensive and uncertain about the support they had for their portfolio work. What happened? Why had two angry parents been able to stir up so much controversy?

There are many possible explanations, but no single explanation will capture the whole story. From our perspective, however, the critical question was not why a tiny group of parents had become upset but, rather, why hadn't other parents felt clear enough about what portfolios were? And why weren't teachers using those parents to rally quickly and effectively in support of the project? It was clear that we had not been thoughtful and committed enough to making the work with portfolios accessible and understandable to parents, the school committee, and the local press. Further, we hadn't been effective in explaining just who we were as outsiders, what kind of "research" were we doing with their kids, and who was in control of the school. In short, we made mistakes and we had to give a lot of thought to handling these matters quite differently in the future.

BUILDING A CULTURE THAT EMBRACES, OR AT LEAST TOLERATES, CHANGE

A risk, by definition, involves doing something that matters with a significant chance for failure. The larger the advantages of success and the cost of failure, the greater the risk. Taking risks in education, especially in classrooms, is a serious undertaking. Experimenting with assessment is important enough to warrant taking risks. Questions about the commitment of precious classroom time, the possibility of asking children to do things that are too difficult for them, the reconsideration of basic conceptions about children's responsibility for their own education and subsequent questions of the teachers' responsibility and authority are all issues that virtually everyone has feelings about—usually very strong feelings.

To make matters more complex, changing classroom practices is not a matter of endless addition. In general, when a new practice is introduced, something else must be sacrificed. Trade-offs are inevitable given the limited time in the school day. But change also implies rejection of something that others still value. So there are difficult choices to make, as well as the risk of coming into direct conflict with the practices and beliefs of others. Conflicts can be quite healthy but they can also be unnerving.

When a new activity involves changing assessment practices, there is a good chance that it will be greeted with some suspicion. Everyone from parents to central office administrators to school committee members and teachers down the hall will want to know about these changes. Portfolio assessment is often especially disturbing. By its nature it questions fundamental assumptions about the evaluation of learning, and the nearly universal use of testing and grading, as well as the basis for teachers' judgments of children's academic performance.

There is also the risk of personal failure for teachers. Trying new activities and approaches in the classroom can be an unsettling experience: It may turn out to be an exhilarating success or a total flop but, most likely, will fall somewhere in between. The success of building structures to support thoughtful, collaborative evaluation of experiments in the classroom is inextricably bound up with the practice of protecting innovation by building a school culture of change and innovation.

Portfolios cannot be implemented without teachers trying new things in the classrooms. The risks can be minimized only when the custom in the school is to experiment with new approaches to curriculum, assessment and pedagogy, when the expectation is that all teachers are trying to improve their teaching all the time, and when there are support and resources for those changes. Building this kind of culture is a long process that involves the entire community within and around the school.

CLOSED DOORS

Most people do the same thing when they are trying something new: They close the door to the room in which the experiment will take place. It is a completely natural instinct to put walls around things one wants to protect. After all, you don't really know if it will work. There may well be a lot of naysayers and critics around. Keep out those who might question or criticize until the work has indisputably proven itself.

However, we have learned that it is precisely at this moment of vulnerability that it is most important to keep the doors open. After two full years of our work with teachers, we realized that we had made sure that teachers talked regularly and openly among themselves about their experiments with portfolios. But we had seriously overlooked the importance of inviting parents and district administrators and school committee members into the classrooms as well. Not all on the same day, of course, and not all in the first week. But all of these people and more have an investment in what happens in classrooms. When we and our collaborating teachers wanted the support of the community for this new work, we found that the previous two years had mostly produced confusion and, to some degree, suspicion and hostility. We had not included them in the process and had almost fatally subverted our own strategy for success.

Closed doors breed suspicion. This is a phenomenon hardly restricted to education or assessment. Recent events in these arenas, notably the response in Pennsylvania to the Department of Education's "outcomes-based education" initiative, remind us of this truth. The New Standards Project, a national organization dedicated to the development of new forms of assessment, has made communication with the public a central part of its program. Having sponsored an extensive study of public opinions about standards in education, New Standards has published a book on strategies for building public engagement with the reform of assessment practices (*Effective Public Engagement*, for copies and reference information call Jill Bateman at 716-546-7620). "The advice here is that you have to continually focus on the community and not take for granted that people are with you." (*The New Standard* 1993).

The impulse to close the doors of the classroom or the school while changes are being implemented is powerful. Teachers do it all the time, but the cost in terms of isolation, suspicion and lack of base support for practices that need resources is enormous.

KEEPING THE DOORS OPEN

We are convinced that the best way to protect innovative practices is to be as open and public as possible. This is not easy. It requires explaining what you are planning and doing, why you are doing it and how you will decide if it is effective. It demands that people's concerns and ideas be heard and seriously considered even if it takes more time and slows down the process of change. It means risking skeptics outside your door (or right in your room!) when things don't go smoothly, waiting to remind you that they never thought your experiment would work. In the end, many more people will be supportive of your work when they have been included in the process along the way. Without taking the risk of opening the doors you will be assured of no support.

Opening classroom doors to share innovative practices does not mean inviting everyone in to tell you what to do. These are occasions for informing and discussing but not for group decision-making. Teachers will never make everyone happy with all of their choices and approaches. The more explicit an explanation for those choices, however, the more likely there will be grounds for understanding, if not embracing. The objections of parents or a colleague's dire warnings of failure must be seriously considered. They may provoke rethinking of some aspect of the innovation, but they must be balanced by the responses of others as well as the evidence emerging in the classroom. Teachers must be confident in their own experiments while having the courage to accept criticism.

This open-door policy applies to school-wide assessment experiments as much as classroom innovations. The policy may be more important when the whole school is moving in new directions. An elementary school principal we spoke with was very supportive of all of the portfolio work her teachers were doing. She acknowledged that the staff was getting ready to do away with grades on the report cards but she was not prepared to allow that change. "We have a lot more work to do with parents before we can make that change. I have to feel sure that every parent is informed and understands why we would want to make that change and what we plan to do that is better than assigning grades. It is simply too big a change to make. There are parents who will think we simply aren't doing our jobs. So we have to talk and talk in groups and one-on-one before we get close to that kind of change.")

WHO TO INVITE IN?

The practice of making classroom experiments and innovations public is not simply an act of opening up and giving. As an atmosphere of support for change builds in a school, the bene-fits of an open-door policy become much more apparent. There are many different groups of people to invite in and different things to get from each of those groups.

Support, approval, different perspectives, unexpected resources and fresh ideas will be forthcoming, even if there is also skepticism, criticism and challenge. At the very least, individual teachers and the staff as a whole will have to clarify their reasons for undertaking these innovations. They will have to become articulate about what they believe and why they believe it. They will also have to acknowledge what is uncertain to them. The goal is to diminish suspicion and distrust.

Parents

Starting with those closest to the children, it is, of course, imperative to inform parents, at the very least, and, at best, engage them with their children's portfolios. Changes in assess-ment practices can be quite confusing to parents. Sometimes those changes bring shifts in the way in which a teacher shows authority and talks about responsibility for learning. These shifts may not seem desirable to all parents. Also, the classroom time given to portfolios may seem inappropriate to some parents, espe-cially if they are concerned about their child's academic perfor-mance. These concerns must be acknowledged and addressed in order for everyone to move forward with comfort and confidence.

In general, from our observations, parents seem delighted to see their child's work collected, protected and considered important enough to return to time and again in an effort to understand the child and her school performance. Parent confer-ences become far less dominated by grade books and far more involved with the actual work the child has produced. The pres-ence of the child is felt in a very different way.

Other Adults in the Building

Within the building, other teachers, administrators, specialists and professional staff need to know what is changing in the school. It can be frustrating and sometimes infuriating to know that colleagues are experimenting with new approaches to assessment and to be left "in the dark" about that work. When there is no structured way to support colleagues, it is frightfully easy to undermine them. Many teachers are painfully familiar with working in an atmosphere of resentment, resistance, apathy and cynicism. Such an environment certainly doesn't encourage individual teachers to try new practices and make bold efforts to improve their teaching.

In order to support innovations, all of the adults in the building need to understand the whys and hows of these changes. One key way to demonstrate support can be describing and explaining these innovations to people outside the building. Everyone doesn't have to agree with every new practice but everyone should defend the right of teachers to experiment and innovate.

At the Shutesbury Elementary School in Massachusetts, the staff took the need to know what was happening in each other's classrooms very seriously. They applied for and received an in-service grant that allowed them to hire substitute teachers so that every teacher could be freed up to visit a number of other classrooms in the building. Everyone visited and everyone hosted. Each visit was preceded and followed up by conversations between the visiting and the hosting teachers.

District Administrators

Within the district but outside the school, there may be a host of people whose professional responsibilities include assessment practices in each school. These people, from district assessment directors to department coordinators to the superintendent and the school committee, have a right and obligation to know about changes in a school's approach to assessment. The superintendent doesn't need to be called in every time a classroom teacher tries a new form of reflection with her students. But if all the teachers in the building are experimenting with portfolios it is certainly wise to inform the superintendent of these developments. The thinking behind these moves, the goals, the plan and ways of evaluating the effectiveness of the changes should be explained. Bitter experience has taught us that it is infinitely better for a superintendent to hear about the use of portfolios first from the teachers implementing them rather than from an angry parent who doesn't understand them.

Concerned Members of the Community

Moving beyond those directly concerned with particular children or a specific school, there are many people who care about young people and education. Identifying those who might have an interest in your work with portfolios is a step to building wider professional and community support. Leaders of community groups, for example, who serve particular populations in a school might be quite interested in new ways of documenting the accomplishments of those youngsters. Business people in the community, especially those who are interested in employing high school graduates are very concerned with the real meaning of a diploma. Senior portfolios can represent a breakthrough in the presentation of a recent graduate's interests, skills and achievements, and an employer's ability to make effective hiring decisions.

Domain Experts

Teachers whose portfolios focus on a specific subject area and who are exploring with their students appropriate criteria for assessment have benefited from inviting professionals in specific fields to join them in the process. On what grounds, for example, should a middle school student's poetry be evaluated? Invite a poet to join in considering this problem. Architects can help consider ways of assessing even very young children's building and design projects. Scientists can offer critical advice to the assessment of scientific experiments and investigations. The perspective of a professional can illustrate how work in that domain is actually assessed in professional settings.

Ron Berger, a sixth grade teacher at the Shutesbury Elementary School, regularly seeks out people from the area with expertise in work that his students are engaged in. Ron has brought in architects, geologists, jewelers, book designers and illustrators, commercial artists and others to meet with his students. These guests are not there simply to lecture; there is always examination and discussion of the work students have produced. The experts help the students develop sensitivity to the standards that exist in the professional world for excellence in their domain. Ron and his students work quite explicitly in applying those standards to their own work. The quality of the work usually improves and the guests generally leave these visits as great fans of the students, their work and the school.

PROVIDING STRUCTURES WHEN THE DOORS ARE OPEN

There are lots of good times to invite people in to hear about work with portfolios. Parent-teacher conferences, open houses and parent nights, celebrations of children's work with student performances—all are occasions that already are part of many schools' calendars. Talking explicitly about portfolios, as a part of these events makes the presence of portfolios part of the expectations parents and children have about school.

Special meetings to talk more generally about portfolios may also have to be scheduled. In one school, special parent nights were devoted to staff and parent discussions of children's work. Everyone met by grades and looked at examples of children's work that weren't from any of the children in those grades at that time. This was the first time many parents looked seriously at the writing of a child who wasn't theirs. Parents' concerns about what is normal and appropriate for a child the age of their son or daughter were addressed more specifically than references to test scores.

The portfolio process is one of education. Portfolios won't make sense to everyone overnight. This process must be approached with all of the thoughtfulness and creativity that would be given to any curriculum. Most people (even those working in schools) have never sat down to read a child's portfolio of work. Reading a body of work from a child is different from almost any other kind of reading. How to do it, what to look for, or what to say when you are done are not obvious skills.

In some schools, teachers introduce the idea of portfolio assessment during open-house evenings for parents. Knowing that most parents are unfamiliar with portfolios, they show them how revealing a portfolio can be about a child's interests, needs and progress. They start by sharing portfolios from other schools and various grade levels. During these sessions, there is plenty of time for parents to raise questions, fears and confusion. While the staff can't address all of their concerns, most parents leave feeling more confident that their perspectives are being considered as the staff moves forward with this new approach.

In later sessions, teachers hold wide-ranging discussions of parents' own experiences of being evaluated as school children, what parents most want to know about their child's experience in school, and parents' and teachers' feelings about current assessment practices. When children finally brought their portfolios home, nearly all of the parents were open, interested and comfortable with the new practice.

If it seems as there is a lot of work in educating the community about portfolios, the perception is accurate. It can be taken on a bit at a time but should be planned strategically. The purpose is to inform and build support. Since resistance to changes in assessment practices is almost inevitable, anticipating that resistance and respecting the sources of it are essential. There will be diverse and often antagonistic positions about how assessment should be practiced in school. The understanding and respect teachers and staff show to those who don't like portfolios will, hopefully, establish a precedent of tolerance and acceptance even when there is still disagreement and frustration.

All of this work can be either greatly facilitated or inhibited by school administrators. Principals who want to help create a culture of change and improvement can provide support in many forms for teachers' efforts to open the doors of their classrooms.

Inviting people in to a classroom to learn about portfolios is time and energy consuming but principals can lend authority to these occasions by showing up, sharing perspectives on reasons for pursuing portfolio assessment and listening and facilitating when people express serious criticism or concern. Teachers must feel that the school administration stands behind their right to experiment with portfolios, even though their principal may not agree with absolutely everything they try.

This is serious and demanding work but it can't be ignored. The cost of ignoring it can be the ability to conduct innovations and experiments at all. The benefits go well beyond portfolio acceptance and into the creation of a community that supports, respects and expects change and innovation.

SUSTAINING INNOVATION

> *Last year's innovation becomes this year's tradition.*
> — *Ray Levi, Principal*

When the work of protecting innovation is successful, Ray's prediction becomes reality. Building a culture of change and innovation around the implementation of portfolios is essential if they are to become the basis for assessments that produce improvements. While using portfolios in every classroom may have significant value in those rooms, that is not enough. As we discussed in the previous chapter on bi-focal assessment, portfolios have the potential to provide evidence of the effectiveness of educational programs. If they are used in this way by a school staff and they lead to new plans for improving different aspects of those programs, change and innovation become an ongoing process.

When protecting innovations and experimentation becomes constant it becomes crucial to figure out ways of sustaining the innovators—the teachers and administrators who design and produce these changes. This work must go on within a school and across schools and communities.

Within the School

As director of The Agnon School in Beachwood, Ohio, Ray Levi has moved with his staff from initiating new approaches to assessment to making sure that those approaches continue to evolve, develop, and serve the needs of children and parents. When he discusses this new stage, Ray is quite clear that a strategy for moving from "protecting initial innovation to sustaining innovation over the long term" must have multiple components.

Ray is quick to point out that a school community is an ever-changing population. New teachers, new students, and new parents enter the community every year. Portfolios are not likely to be familiar to all of those new to the community and each of these groups will have different relationships to and responsibilities with them. How, then, to introduce newcomers to them? And how to keep work with portfolios evolving for those students and teachers who have already been working with them?

There are countless strategies to use. A brief look at some of Ray's approaches to these challenges provides a useful starting point for considering these questions. Focusing on parents' confusion and concerns, Ray initiated evening meetings in which issues of assessment could be discussed openly with lots of information and many examples. Ray also brought outsiders, including Project Zero staff, in for these meetings to provide a broader context for the work the Agnon staff was undertaking. These meetings also helped to establish a working vocabulary that parents, staff and children can use. (It is as important to be sure that there is clarity in talking with parents as it is in conversations among the staff. Often parents feel intimidated and less welcome when staff uses language that is unclear. If you've never seen an elementary schooler's portfolio, it is hard to be enthusiastic about the fact that your child is keeping one. Very few parents of school-age children today had any personal experience with portfolios in their schooling.) The staff created a glossary of assessment terms as a reference for parents.

Ray also established an assessment policy committee that includes various members of the wider school community. This group issued a policy statement that outlines the philosophical basis of assessment practice in the school. The statement provides both parents and staff with a common reference point to refer to and debate.

The Agnon staff is actively encouraged to get out of the school and see for themselves what others are doing and thinking about assessment. Ray frequently has teachers attend conferences and visit other schools. He also encourages other educators to visit Agnon. At times, his staff go out as seekers and students looking for new ideas and then, alternately, they go out as consultants and conference presenters.

A sustained, varied and all-out effort is required to keep this work vital and evolving. But, says Ray, "ultimately, it is the portfolios and the students behind them that will sustain innovation." The quality of the work in the portfolios, the degree to which they reflect active and exciting learning by students, and students' investment in their own learning are the elements on which the fate of these assessments finally rest.

Across Schools and Communities

In the second year of our research, we realized that much of what sustained our enthusiasm for work with portfolios was our unique position. We traveled from school to school, seeing the results, sometimes confusing, occasionally frustrating and often exhilarating, of many teachers' work. But none of the teachers we worked with had this advantage. They didn't have the benefit of sitting in another teacher's classroom or of pouring over portfolios from another school. They didn't get to see how it was done in other places or if other people had the same problems, or what their strategies were for coping with those problems. They didn't get to see that in some cases they had solved problems that others hadn't. In short, isolation within a school as well as within a classroom was a serious problem.

As a result we initiated two projects. First, we established the New England Regional Assessment Network. We invited teachers we were working with to come to our offices for a day of conversation and sharing. This was strictly volunteer and off-school hours. There were no big speeches from researchers and no workshops on how to do some aspect of portfolio work. All sessions, large and small, were for discussion and sharing. Topics were chosen and questions agreed upon for the sessions. We facilitated the sessions and gave basic shape to the agenda but there was always plenty of room for adjustment. The network was not designed as professional development in the classic in-service sense. It was a time for teachers to talk with each other about their work with portfolios, problems they encountered, and solutions they invented.

We have had four meetings, twice yearly, and have expanded to include a dinner meeting the night before the Saturday session. The number of participants grows each time and teachers are beginning to pick up conversations with each other just where they left off six months earlier. One of the most interesting developments of this network is the amount of visiting that has gone on between schools. Teachers have been given permission or, in some cases, just taken personal days, to visit other network schools. Sometimes small groups from one school have gone to another and then reciprocal visits are made.

In one case, a whole class of sixth-graders traveled nearly all the way across Massachusetts to spend several days visiting another class of sixth-graders. In addition to soccer and dinner and exploring the town, students brought their portfolios and shared them. In both schools, the teachers had arranged for their graduating students to make presentations of their portfolios to the local middle school teachers. This visit was used as a chance for all of the kids to rehearse their presentations for each other.

Part of our design of the New England Regional Assessment Network was to make the meetings accessible. Although we have some out-of-towners who join us for these meetings, most participants live within a two-hour driving distance, making it possible to come in for the day. Keeping the network regional also facilitates visiting between sessions. The model is rather simple and could be replicated in other regions. Some of our colleagues in Ohio have established a similar network called the Ohio Regional Portfolio Assessment Network (ORPAN). They have had three meetings and, at the last meeting, there were more than 70 participants. They run on a shoestring budget and hope to raise some funds to help sustain the operation.

Our second major initiative was the establishment of a library of portfolios. We have collected more than 30 portfolios from at least a dozen schools, representing mostly elementary and middle grades. We get permission to make facsimile copies of the portfolios we borrow and return the originals to the creators. In addition to the research opportunities inherent in this collection, we are able to make these portfolios available to teachers who are considering working with portfolios and those who want to expand or improve their own current portfolio designs. The portfolios are used in workshops and by teachers who visit Project Zero. As with the regional assessment network, the library is a way to bring the work of teachers and students in one school into other schools, providing models, inspiration, and challenge.

THREE QUESTIONS THAT WON'T GO AWAY

This book about anticipating and preparing for the challenges and obstacles of implementing portfolio assessment teeters on the edge of making those challenges seem overwhelming. Our intention, of course, is to make work with portfolios easier. But our purpose also is for that work to become as varied, useful and rich as possible and to increase its chances of survival.

The implementation of a new form of assessment is one way of changing a school. Since schools are complex and dynamic organisms, changes of one element influence and necessarily produce changes in others. (Unless, of course, the initial changes are superficial or so rigorously separated that they have no bearing on the whole.)

To make real changes, there are questions that won't quit. These questions remain because there aren't simple answers and, ultimately, the answers must be arrived at in the context of particular schools.

1. Where does a school begin?
2. Do all schools have to incorporate all of these practices?
3. Is a teacher (or a few teachers) ready to start work with portfolios if the staff isn't prepared (or interested) to sign on as a whole?

Answers to these questions lead to a few basic principles:

- It matters less where you start only that you start at a point or with an issue or practice that seems important to you.
- You can be modest with the steps you take or you can decide the best way to go is with dramatic changes. It is important that you have persuasive reasons to believe that you can be successful with whatever steps you take.
- You don't need the entire staff to start working with portfolios. If that were the case few schools would ever take the step. But the ultimate impact of the work is enhanced by the involvement of more and more staff members. Initially informing other staff members about what some people are doing with portfolios is better than keeping that work a secret (unless, of course, there is administrative hostility to portfolios).

As the use of portfolios spreads and schools become places where the things children make are highly valued, we anticipate changes that will be quite pleasing to children. When students do work in school or bring papers or projects in from home, their work will be given serious attention not only from their teachers. Teachers, in fact, may become the organizers of assessments and critiques, exhibitions and judging panels, and debates about the quality and significance of work. They will organize gallery shows and performances, publishing parties and cast parties, community forums and press conferences when major works are shared with the public.

In short, the things children make will take center stage and, under different kinds of light and to various audiences, will be presented for response. Children will look at the work of their peers. Parents and administrators, younger and older children, community members and experts in appropriate fields will all come to the school to see what is being made. They will look at the work and in the work will see the results of both the child and the school. Sometimes the response will be rigorous and demanding and sometimes celebratory. Certainly all children should experience both, as should all teachers.

Part Four

BEFORE THE PRACTICES

Chapter Seven summarizes Project Zero's ten years of research into the use of portfolios in schools. This review explores the relationship between our history of research on children's development in artistic domains, our work with schools implementing portfolios, and the evolution of these portfolio practices.

Chapter 7

PORTFOLIO RESEARCH AT PROJECT ZERO

Research on assessment at Project Zero began in the arts and now spans different kinds of disciplines, grade levels, and school organizations. The focus of this research has always been on judging student learning through careful review of their work. "Portfolios," an idea taken from the arts, is the latest embodiment of this philosophy.

TWO PROJECTS, EIGHT YEARS

This book describes results of the research conducted at Project Zero. This chapter describes the methods we used and what we found in eight years of work.

Two projects are reviewed. From 1985 to 1990, Arts PROPEL focused on assessment in the arts as the first foray into portfolio research at Project Zero. The APPLE project, from 1988 to 1993 used much of what we had learned in PROPEL and brought it to the regular classroom. In describing both, we will talk about lessons learned rather than research findings.

In a sense, our research plots a line between two points. One point is the reality of what exists in schools and the other is a description of what could be in the future; the line is our plan for getting from here to there. During the course of both research projects, we worked intensively in schools. We interviewed teachers and children, administrators and parents. We observed meetings and classrooms. We videotaped children at work. We conducted workshops and participated in meetings. We arranged visits and contacts between schools in order to connect teachers with shared concerns. We wrote field notes, transcribed tapes, watched videotapes, discussed what we were observing as a research team. We challenged one another, argued, read, consulted with colleagues doing comparable work, and compiled reports. Through this collaborative activity, new ideas emerged. And as soon as these ideas were articulated, we looked for ways to test them, or to talk them over. In this collaborative development, our team kept naming and renaming questions and positing possible answers. This book is the result of our work.

ARTS PROPEL

The Arts PROPEL project began with a grant from the Rockefeller Foundation to explore assessment in visual art, music, and imaginative writing. Project Zero was joined in this effort by researchers from the Educational Testing Service and teachers and administrators in the Pittsburgh Public Schools. Over the course of the five-year project, the research team developed tools for assessment that were built around structured projects and student portfolios.

Arts PROPEL pioneered two innovative assessment techniques. Domain projects were classroom activities in which students tackled problems similar to those undertaken by practicing artists, such as singing a familiar song in different styles. Portfolio techniques in Arts PROPEL were developed to capture the history of the student's learning process in these projects. A portfolio in the visual arts, for example, might include initial sketches for a portrait, experiments in different media, mistakes and corrections, and notes from famous portraits that provided inspiration and ideas, as well as the final portrait itself. These portfolios were not tucked away and forgotten, but kept alive as a source of instruction through periodic review. By using portfolios this way, students learned to internalize artistic standards and apply them to their own work.

Lessons from PROPEL

Several lessons emerged for teachers of all subjects from this work. First, we became convinced that new assessment practices can be designed through thoughtful collaboration between teachers and researchers. Bringing curriculum and assessment closer together in the day-to-day work of the classroom can only be accomplished by the teacher; but adding a strong critical element—observing, documenting, and analyzing these experiences—became the role for researchers.

Through Arts PROPEL and other arts education research initiatives at Project Zero, we also began to realize that there are important lessons for all of education that can be drawn from the arts. For example, in the arts there are no reliable tests. Teachers in the arts rely strictly on careful judgment of student work, which might be a painting, a composition, or a performance. Furthermore, student work in the arts is important and interesting. Even musical exercises or practice drawings or even the very first efforts of novices are in some ways aesthetic and must be evaluated as such. In short, in the arts, assessment is a part of the creative process, not something that is separated.

Student Work at the Center of Assessment

In the arts, assessment is built around the work and that work is important in itself. This is quite different from assessment in an examination. Examination is important because it reveals the mastery of particular skills, understanding specific concepts, completing some course of study. Art work is authentic but the examination is not. Art works are displayed but examinations are reported only as statistics. Artists and musicians make constant judgments of quality and these judgments are based entirely on an examination of the piece or the performance. The work speaks for itself. Artists or musicians do not create end-of-chapter tests to determine where they stand; they know how to look and listen.

Arts PROPEL was designed with this fact in mind—that the authenticity of an art work significantly changes the process of assessment. Arts PROPEL found that even with beginning students, whose work was immature or imperfect, the authenticity of that work allowed it to be evaluated on its own terms. The work of the beginning art student or musician is just as authentic as that of the master. The evaluation of that work and of the underlying competencies are very similar.

Assessment: When?

Arts PROPEL also revealed another issue of assessment—timing. Examinations are given at the end of the chapter; performances are evaluated at the end of long periods of practice. However, when these final judgments are the only evaluations, they are seriously inadequate; judgments at the end cannot inform the educational experiences that led up to them.

Here again, the arts are instructive. In a studio art class, the teacher roams about the room, peering over shoulders of students, making suggestions and corrections; the music teacher sits with individual students weekly or daily, listening, suggesting, correcting. Both teachers are deeply involved in assessment of the students, moment to moment, and when the student hangs work in a display or performs for an audience, neither the teachers nor the students are surprised by the outcome. This is very different from a surprising grade on a chapter test. Furthermore, during the regular lessons and critique, as students adjust and improve their capabilities, they also learn to make the necessary discriminations for themselves. They gradually learn to become their own critics.

Reflection

Arts PROPEL developed many techniques to encourage students to critique their own work as part of the assessment process. It coined the term "reflection" to capture these techniques and it found that through systematic reflection students became increasingly sophisticated in their self-critical abilities.

Furthermore, the benefits were considerable: Once students began to critique themselves efficiently, all of their efforts, both working with the teacher and working alone, became more productive. Their sense of themselves, as artists, as creators, as owners of their work, increased as well.

Arts PROPEL also discovered that one of the features of effective reflection was the structured conversations that it sparked. The language of critique quickly became part of the culture of the classroom, with teacher and students freely sharing opinions on a regular basis. Again, the contrast with traditional assessment is instructive. In a reflective classroom with its continuing, open critique, the final judgment is much less important than the sequence of critiques that bring about meaningful changes in the work and in the skills required for that work. Assessment is a continuous, thoughtful, self-referential process, not one that is originates in the one-time judgment of an expert.

The lesson from the Arts PROPEL project is that assessment in the arts is critical to learning, especially when that learning focuses on deep understanding. Arts PROPEL demonstrated that the technique of capturing reflective assessment was possible, especially when its importance to learning was fully understood. Furthermore, students are quite capable at making reflective judgments about their work and they are eager to engage in this process of self-assessment. In the Arts PROPEL work, assessment evolved. It was no longer a technique for maintaining control or simply a process of accountability; it had become an instrument of genuine engagement, and the secret to that transformation was the act of taking seriously what students had produced.

THE APPLE PROJECT

With support from the Lilly Endowment, we continued our work on alternatives to tests with a project called Assessment of Projects and Portfolios for Learning (APPLE). Building on the lessons learned in Arts PROPEL, the APPLE team began to explore how portfolios could be used in regular elementary and middle school classrooms. APPLE looked at how different media, like videotape, audio tape, photography, color photocopying, and computer images, might document and archive student portfolio work.

In building on Arts PROPEL, the APPLE project made two critical shifts. First, it focused its attention on classrooms with a project-based curriculum in non-arts classes. Second, it examined clusters of collaborating teachers and even entire school faculty, instead of individuals working alone.

Portfolios in Project-Based Classrooms

In paying special attention to the project-centered curriculum, APPLE was a logical extension of Arts PROPEL. In the arts classroom the project approach is quite natural; the studio class in visual arts, the ensemble practicing for a performance, or the playwriting workshop are all built around projects. Arts PROPEL built on this tradition with its domain projects and it demonstrated that the portfolio approach fit quite easily in this hands-on environment. The APPLE team found that projects in these non-arts classrooms are less a part of the tradition and, in fact, imply a reconsideration of the necessary pedagogy and, to some extent, a shift in the curriculum itself.

We use the term project-centered to describe classrooms where activity is much less focused on workbooks and isolated seat work. The emphasis is on longer-term assignments involving fairly complex and often interesting tasks. For example, in a project-based classroom, history projects tend to involve work with primary sources and related raw materials. They ask students to identify basic questions, make their own interpretations based on evidence, and share what they have learned through discussion, argumentation, and formal presentation. Students might display the results of their work through verbal or dramatic presentations, written reports, and three-dimensional models.

Like whole language, process writing, and other curriculum innovations, the project-centered approach need not be all-or-nothing. We had the opportunity to watch teachers experiment with these ideas, allowing their teaching practices to transform gradually, rather than making dramatic shifts. Teachers often begin by having their students do a single project during the year. Building on that experience, the teachers then expand to several projects the following year.

In any case, a curriculum designed around projects raises serious questions about traditional assessment techniques. For example, many teachers find that what their students are learning in projects cannot be examined easily. Certainly, after doing a project, students can be given a test of their factual knowledge, but projects develop many other skills beyond facts. Using resource materials, investigating questions over an extended period, organizing a small group, and meeting deadlines are accomplishments that are not likely to be reflected in a traditional chapter test. The challenge is to create a new assessment that reflects more completely the competencies and skills learned through project work.

Making Portfolios a School-Wide Activity

The second shift of APPLE was from the portfolio system as a classroom activity to a school-wide activity. PROPEL worked with the arts specialists in a particular school and the resulting portfolio techniques were viewed as "arts assessment." APPLE moved these ideas into the mainstream classrooms where they became part of the grading system, influenced parent conferences, and informed school-wide accountability.

It quickly became apparent that the portfolio assessment system was not a simple classroom exercise but that it must eventually involve an entire school and school-wide conversations. We found that the proper environment for portfolios is the school. We believe that if schools can successfully build portfolio cultures then these conversations naturally spill over beyond schools to create community-wide portfolio systems as well.

Two questions guided the APPLE research: 1) What are effective ways to assess student work on complex and extensive projects over the course of the entire school year? 2) Given an assessment system that accomplishes this, what does it take to implement that system throughout the school, and make it stick?

With respect to the first question, we found that portfolios fulfill the promise as an effective assessment tool of project work, but they create new challenges around the issues of documentation, selection, reflection and self-assessment. The question of sustained implementation underscores the fact that this undertaking is a school-wide issue, one that requires the collective effort of the entire staff of the school. Indeed, we believe that the greatest threat to sustained portfolio assessment is the failure to recognize the implications for all the teachers in the school. While individual teachers can accomplish the mechanics of keeping portfolios, working alone they often fail to figure out how to evaluate the results.

They ask us: How do I use this to inform my practice? How do I share the results with my colleagues? What happens if our judgments are very different? If portfolios are to take root as a useful and effective assessment, it requires the development of school-wide answers to these questions.

The Research of APPLE

Our research with APPLE into portfolio practice is based on our work with about 50 classroom teachers. Since their experiences are critical to the narrative, in this section we will describe how we worked together—a set of activities that might loosely be termed "research." We also describe briefly what we learned.

In education, research often consists of the experimental pursuit of an hypothesis. Our work however, was influenced by non-experimental methods, such as ethnography, portraiture, case studies, and action research. Taking an observational stance helped us work in schools in constructive and collaborative relationships. We were able to participate in the changes and document and analyze the results.

First, we conducted this research by invitation—that is, we were invited by teachers or school faculty to collaborate with them as they began to make changes in assessment. As a true collaboration, we did not function simply as detached observers. In the spirit of action research, our purpose from the start was to work actively with these schools to develop new practices, to observe and document the outcomes, and to report what we learned.

Second, we established collaboration in this research as a priority. The teachers originally sought us out as the "experts" who could provide them with perspective and candid feedback. As researchers we sought out teachers who could bring classroom expertise to the enterprise. From the beginning it was essential that we find and maintain a balance in our teaching and learning relationships.

The difficulty and the importance of balance was dramatized in one brief interaction at a teachers' meeting in a school where we had been working for two years. The group was struggling with a particularly knotty assessment question. The frustration grew until finally one teacher blurted out, "Oh, wait, I get it! You guys really don't have the answers!" Even after two years of hard, honest work with us, this teacher had held onto the notion that we had answers to their questions but were unwilling, for some reason, to share them.

Our role in these schools was an active one. We offered perspective when it seemed necessary. We shared the experiences of other schools to provide models and alternative approaches. We arranged visits and conversations across schools. We provided the perspective of findings from other educational researchers. We questioned the theoretical foundations of current and new practices. We constantly asked, "Why are you doing what you are doing the way you are doing it?" We participated in negotiating the rate and sequence of changes, sometimes arguing for going slower and other times suggesting a faster pace.

A central part of responsible collaborations is to keep asking, "So, what's the big idea?" In other words, what are the theoretical underpinnings of what we are doing? What ideas are we basing our practices on? These may be theories of human development, learning, intelligence, organizational change, group dynamics, or cognition. And they may have been derived by individuals through observation and thought or by researchers through large-scale, long-term studies. The source doesn't matter. The important part is to be cognizant and public about the ideas that are informing and justifying practice. We tried to raise these questions and participate in articulating answers.

At the same time, however, we always recognized that our agenda and timetable had to be subordinate to those of the collaborating school. While we began with many ideas about what could happen, or even ideas about what should happen during this collaboration, we did not impose those ideas on the schools. Developing new forms of assessment is a serious undertaking, one that touches directly the values and the deep interests and goals that each community has for its children. As researchers and outsiders, our perspective was only one of many, and imposing our values would have been both inappropriate and unproductive.

After several years of working in very different schools, each with a distinct timetable and agenda, we began to analyze our experiences, looking across the different schools for patterns and parallels, always assuming that there might be significant differences in the ways in which various schools implement portfolio assessment. No two schools started in exactly the same place, nor did they proceed at the same pace. No school worked on all of these issues at the same time and absolutely none of our collaborators followed all of our advice.

In our research, we looked for the patterns and commonalties among many differences. What is similar is that all of our collaborating teachers are moving away from workbooks and classrooms in which students work alone at their desks. The emphasis is shifting to complex tasks that include elements of work authentic to a domain. History projects, for example, tend to involve work with a variety of sources, especially primary sources, and involve naming questions and making interpretations based on evidence. There is often a variety of ways in which students can display what they have learned—verbal or dramatic presentations, written reports, models—through their investigations.

And what did we find through these investigations? First, we learned that the process of transforming assessment practices is not a one-time activity. It cannot be accomplished by a decree from the superintendent. It is not implemented after a two-day in-service for the staff in September nor is it in place after a year devoted to setting standards and establishing benchmarks. Transforming assessment requires a long-term, on-going, multifaceted effort that can take several years before significant and visible changes are evident.

New forms of assessment that fit the program and values of a school must be developed and designed by those most involved in that school. That development begins with the analysis of current practices and the negotiation of a coherent statement of educational goals. It requires patience, experimentation, consideration of new practices, and so on. Like every other aspect of any educational program, the strategies for assessment must be evaluated regularly and continually if they are to remain useful and healthy.

We also found that because of the many demands on a school staff—from the district office, from changes in students' lives, from new program decisions—that even with a deep commitment to implementing portfolios, a school may not have the luxury of giving that work the sustained attention it needs. Our research suggests that two to three years of initial focus on portfolios is crucial for significant and lasting progress to be made. This is often simply not possible in the real world of schools. Only school personnel know when to shift the portfolio work to the back burner and when to bring the assessment work forward again.

BIBLIOGRAPHY

Balm, S. 1995. Using Portfolio Assessment in a Kindergarten Classroom. *Teaching and Change*, 2(2): 141-151.

Breivik, P.S. and Senn, J.A. 1997. *Information Literacy: Educating Children for the 21st Century*. 2nd edition. Washington, D.C.: NEA Professional Library.

Duckworth, E. 1987. *The Having of Wonderful Ideas and Other Essays on Teaching and Learning*. New York: Teachers College Press.

Gardner, H. 1991. *The Unschooled Mind; How Children Think and How Schools Should Teach*. New York: Basic Books.

———— 1990. Assessment in Context: The Alternative to Standardized Testing. In *Changing Assessments: Alternative Views of Aptitude, Achievement, and Instruction*, B. Gifford and M.C. O'Connor, eds. Boston: Kluwer Publishers.

Gray, L., et al. 1996. *Multiple Intelligences*. Washington, D.C.: NEA Professional Library.

Grosvenor, L., et al. 1993. *Student Portfolios*. Washington, D.C.: NEA Professional Library.

Jervis, K. 1996. *Eyes on the Child: Three Portfolio Stories*. New York: Teachers College Press.

Kochendorfer, L. 1994. *Becoming a Reflective Teacher*. Washington, D.C.: NEA Professional Library.

Lescher, M. 1995. *Portfolios: Assessing Learning in the Primary Grades*. Washington, D.C.: NEA Professional Library.

Lyman, L., Foyle, H., and Azwell, T. 1993. *Assessing Cooperative Learning Through Portfolios. Cooperative Learning in the Elementary Classroom*. Washington, D.C.: NEA Professional Library.

McTighe, J. and Ferrara, S. 1994. *Assessing Learning in the Classroom*. Washington, D.C.: NEA Professional Library.

New Standards 1993. Listening to the Public. *The New Standard*, 1(3).

Walters, J., Seidel, S., and Gardner, H. 1994. Children as Reflective Practitioners: Bringing Metacognition to the Classroom. In *Creating Powerful Thinking in Teachers and Students: Diverse Perspectives*, C. Collins-Block and J. Mangieri, eds. Fort Worth: Harcourt Brace.

Welch, D. 1995. Improving Student Performance Through Alternative Assessment. *Teaching and Change*, 2(4): 369-391.